The Ascent of Vishnu and the Fall of Brahma

The Ascent of Vishnu and the Fall of Brahma

The Galaxy of Hindu Gods
Book 2

SWAMI ACHUTHANANDA

Copyright © 2018 Swami Achuthananda

All rights reserved. No part of this book may be reproduced or transmitted in any form or by any means, electronic or mechanical, including photocopying, recording, or by an information storage or retrieval system, without the written permission of the author, except for the inclusion of brief quotations in a review.

The author can be contacted at *swamia@mmmgh.com*

Editor: Polly Kummel, *www.amazinphrasin.com*
Page Layout and Design: *Wordzworth.com*
Cover Design: Cathi Stevenson, *www.BookCoverExpress.com*
Photo Credit: *www.depositphotos.com* and public domain (Wikimedia Commons)

ISBN: 978-0-9757883-3-2

Relianz Communications Pty Ltd,
Queensland 4035, Australia.
Email: *contact@relianz.com.au*

Other books by Swami Achuthananda:
Many Many Many Gods of Hinduism
(A Concise Introduction to Hinduism)

Volumes in **The Galaxy of Hindu Gods** series:
Book One: The Reign of the Vedic Gods
Book Two: The Ascent of Vishnu and the Fall of Brahma
Book Three: Rama and the Early Avatars of Vishnu
Book Four: Krishna and the Later Avatars of Vishnu
Book Five: The Awesome and Fearsome Shiva
Book Six: Devi—Goddesses from Devious Kali to Divine Lakshmi
Book Seven: Bhagavad Gita—An Odyssey of Self-Discovery

*Dedicated to my sister,
the quintessential bhakta*

Contents

Chapter 1	The Beginning of the World	1
Chapter 2	Brahma – The Creator God	5
Chapter 3	A Day of Brahma	11
Chapter 4	Manu and the Flood Myth	17
Chapter 5	Trimurti – The Hindu Triad	21
Chapter 6	Brahman – The Ultimate Reality	25
Chapter 7	The Churning of the Milky Ocean	29
Chapter 8	Who Among the Gods is the Greatest?	35
Chapter 9	Vishnu – The Preserver God	39
Chapter 10	Alexander Conquers India and Retreats	47
Chapter 11	The Renaissance of Hinduism	51
Chapter 12	Vishnu Sahasranama – The Thousand Names of Vishnu	59
Chapter 13	How Dhruva Became the Unwavering Polaris	63
Chapter 14	Bhakti Sweeps India	67
Chapter 15	The Abode of Gods – Temples	73
Chapter 16	Vaishnavism – The Most Dominant Sect of Hinduism	79
Chapter 17	Vishnu Is Not Easy to Impress	83
Chapter 18	Anatomy of a Hindu Temple	87
Chapter 19	Angkor Wat – The Mother of All Temples	91
Chapter 20	Exploring Mythology Through Paintings	97
Chapter 21	Andal – The Girl Who Ruled Over the Lord	105

Chapter 22	Are You the Scientific Type?	109
Chapter 23	Ragamala – A Garland of Melodies	113
Chapter 24	Mira Bai – The Princess Who Became a Saint	119
Chapter 25	Devotion is Superior to Erudition	125
Chapter 26	Char Dham Yatra – A Pilgrimage of a Lifetime	131
Index		135
What's Next?		145

Dear Reader,

If you come across a Hindu on the street, chances are she's a Vaishnava. That's no sheer coincidence since three-fifths of all Hindus are Vaishnavas; that is, devotees of Vishnu or his various incarnations, such as Rama and Krishna. The Hare Krishnas who brighten busy streets with their chanting and dancing also belong to this sect. That said, Vaishnavas may also worship other gods and goddesses, although their primary object of devotion is Vishnu or his many forms. Scholars call this form of worship henotheism—not polytheism.[1] In fact worshipping many deities is typical of most Hindu sects.

Vishnu occupies a dominant place in the Hindu pantheon. Known to be a gentlemanly god, he's the most lovable of the members of the Trimurti and full of mercy. So you want to ace an exam or secure the best paying job? Okay, head to the nearest Vishnu temple and empty your savings at the temple coffers, right? If you were to take this route, chances are you may fail the exam or ruin your employment prospects for a long time. Why? I am afraid Vishnu is not the god to consult for matters that require instant gratification. That's because token worship does not please Vishnu, who has been known to put his devotees through severe hardships before showering them with blessings. The story of Kuchela[2] amplifies this peculiar trait of Vishnu. Vishnu once denied even his ardent devotee Narada his wish. (We describe this story in this book.)

Although Vishnu, the preserver of the universe, is an important deity in India, he maintained a low profile during the Vedic period. In fact he was so low key that Brahma, the creator god, became more prominent toward the end of Vedic times. Scholars believe that for a time Brahma was the most powerful deity. But Brahma's luster faded as Vishnu and Shiva gained significance and attracted more followers. Mythology is teeming with stories that explain why Brahma lost stature. Scholars also

---

[1] Henotheism is the worship of one god without denying the existence of other gods.
[2] The story of Kuchela is described in book 4 of this series.

believe that during this power transition, the myths originally attributed to Brahma were adapted to Vishnu. And Vishnu's numerous avatars, Rama and Krishna in particular, further accelerated his popularity. By the way, the concept of avatar is a specialty of Vishnu when he turns into a cosmic undercover law enforcement agent to maintain law and order in the universe.

After the Vedic period a major shift took place in Hindus' form of worship. Worship through bhakti (devotion to a particular god) was considered superior to making sacrifices or doing penance. In this book—the second in *The Galaxy of Hindu Gods* series—we take a closer look at the ascent of Vishnu and the decline of Brahma. We also dissect bhakti in detail. If the first book was about sacrifice, this book is about bhakti.

We will also describe pivotal mythological events during this period, such as the churning of the milky ocean (*samudra manthan*) and the creation myths. Although Hindu mythology has many stories about how the world came into being, we'll begin with a popular version that finds Brahma enclosed in a lotus that is sprouting from the naval of Vishnu, who in turn is reclining in his famous Ananda Sayana posture. In case you are not familiar with this pose, this is pretty much the same position we adopt while watching TV from the couch, with the remote control replacing Vishnu's conch shell. The concepts of *manvantaras* and the cycles of creation—a fascination for the late American scientist Carl Sagan—are also introduced in this book.

No real journey takes place without detours. At times we will take a broader view of mythology by examining temple architecture, paintings, and other artifacts of the past. If you have noticed the differences in temples in northern and southern India, you will learn why. Classical music also is different in northern and southern India. Furthermore, ancient paintings and sculptures provide insights about deities but only if you look closely. Although early paintings are never perfect— often filtered by the sources and distorted by the ravages of time—they present the beliefs of a bygone era. Above all they provide a cornucopia of information that deepen our understanding of the culture and heritage of ancient India.

Swami Achuthananda (Sach)

Vishnu in the Ananda Sayana position

1

The Beginning of the World

The creation of a thousand forests is in one acorn.

—RALPH WALDO EMERSON, 1803-1882

"Ksheera sagara sayana …," so goes a famous Carnatic song that describes in glowing words Vishnu reclining on an ocean of milk. The song alludes to the recumbent form of Vishnu relaxing carefree on a sea of milk with his wife, Lakshmi, by his side—which has important consequences to our universe, as we will see shortly.[3] While Shiva's explosive dance (*tandava*) has a neutron-bomb effect and is the precursor of the end of the universe, Vishnu's cosmic sleep (*sayana*) announces the beginning of a new world.

---

[3] The song was composed by the 18th century prolific composer Tyagaraja. Like other forms of Indian art, Carnatic music is said to be of divine origin and steeped in the scriptures of Vedas. It is the system of music prevalent in the southern part of India, comprising the states of Andhra Pradesh, Karnataka, Kerala, and Tamil Nadu. Traditional Indian classical music consists of both Carnatic and Hindustani music. Like Carnatic music, Hindustani also evolved from ancient Hindu traditions, but emerged as a distinct form as a result of Persian and Islamic influences.

THE ASCENT OF VISHNU AND THE FALL OF BRAHMA

Hinduism has many creation myths. One popular version speaks of the time when no heaven or earth existed, just a vast ocean of milk on which Vishnu is fast asleep, floating atop a giant cobra called Ananda Shesha. The numerous coils of the serpent serve as Vishnu's foam mattress, while its one thousand hoods form a canopy that protects the dreaming deity. Seated next to Vishnu is Lakshmi, who is lovingly massaging his feet.

In this creation myth the night has ended and dawn is about to break. From the depths of the ocean the hum of Om begins to emerge like the drone of millions of bees. A magnificent lotus, several times larger than the giant Russian sunflower, grows out of Vishnu's navel. Hidden within the petals is the god Brahma. He has been appointed the architect of earth's solar system. But Vishnu is still sleeping, and Brahma has to wait for him to wake up before starting the massive task of creating the solar system. When Lakshmi lifts the veil of unconsciousness from this cosmic intelligence called Vishnu, Brahma can proceed with the act of creation.

Vishnu in Ananda Sayana with Brahma sprouting
from his navel in a lotus; Lakshmi is at Vishnu's feet

THE BEGINNING OF THE WORLD

Having obtained the green light from Vishnu, Brahma enthusiastically splits the lotus into three pieces. He stretches one part into the heavens, another part into earth, and the third part into the skies. Soon Brahma starts using the debris from past cycles of creation and destruction to shape a sun, a moon, and several planets. He creates grass, flowers, trees, and plants of all kinds. He creates the birds and animals. He also gives life to several subtle bodies that were asleep for eons and left over from the last incarnation of the solar system. Earth is soon bristling with life.

If Brahma is the creator of the solar system, Vishnu is the lord of the Milky Way, our galaxy of about 200 billion stars, including the sun. In Hindu cosmology the universe is perpetually in flux. Space and time are cyclical. The universe is created, destroyed, and re-created in repetitive cycles that are never ending. The time between creation and destruction is 8.64 billion years, which corresponds to one day and night of Brahma. According to Hinduism, a universe endures for 4.32 billion years (one day of Brahma), and is then destroyed by natural elements like fire or water. When that happens, Brahma goes to sleep for a night that lasts 4.32 billion human years. The dissolution at the end of each day of Brahma is called *pralaya*. Hindus believe that the *pralaya* repeats every day for the entire lifetime of Brahma—which is one hundred Brahma years, or 311,040 billion human years. (Later we'll tell you how we got this number.) Shiva's drumbeat marks the end of Brahma and our world. After Brahma's death, another 100 Brahma years must elapse before a new Brahma is born and the whole process starts over.

Like Brahma, Vishnu and Shiva will be born again—but on even longer time frames. The lifetime of Vishnu is 37,324,800 trillion years, whereas Shiva lives for 671,846,400 quadrillion years. Fascinating so far? We'll look again at the time frames when we take a closer look at Brahma.

By now you may be thinking that Brahma is doing the hard work, whereas Vishnu and Lakshmi have barely broken a sweat. That's true so far, but once creation is complete, Vishnu takes on the more formidable task of maintaining law and order in the cosmos. And Lakshmi is

THE ASCENT OF VISHNU AND THE FALL OF BRAHMA

Seventh-century sandstone relief of Brahma emerging from Vishnu's navel

no subservient Indian wife, standing by her husband and waggling her head from side to side. She's the power (Shakti) behind Vishnu's action, something that we will discuss later in this series.

> *It is interesting that Hindus, when they speak of the creation of the universe, do not call it the work of God, they call it the play of God, the Vishnulila, lila meaning "play." And they look upon the whole manifestation of all the universes as a play, as a sport, as a kind of dance—lila perhaps being somewhat related to our word lilt.*
>
> —ALAN WATTS, 1915-1973

2

Brahma – The Creator God

Toward the end of the Vedic period, Brahma catapulted to power. Considered the first of the gods, the quad-faced Brahma is the creator and the architect of earth's solar system. He served as Prajapati (the lord of creatures) in Vedic times, but now he, along with Vishnu and Shiva, is a member of the famous Trimurti. (We'll elaborate on the concept of Trimurti in a later chapter.) Burma,[4] the traditional name of the Southeast Asian nation now officially known as Myanmar, is derived from Brahma. The Hebrew patriarch Abraham shows similarity to Brahma, something first observed by 16th century scholars.[5] Although he is equal to Vishnu and Shiva in power and stature, Brahma is the least worshipped member of the triad, even though he's the easiest one to please. Why? He is said to have lost his following because of a single act of wantonness.

---

[4] Medieval texts refer to the nation of Burma as Brahma-desa.

[5] Since the 16th century, scholars have noticed similarities not only between Abraham and Brahma but also between their respective wives, Sarah and Saraswati. The French philosopher Voltaire believed Abraham was descended from the numerous Brahmin priests that left India to disseminate their teachings.

THE ASCENT OF VISHNU AND THE FALL OF BRAHMA

There are many versions of Brahma's origin. One account describes him as self-born when Brahman, the Supreme Being, united with Maya, his energy. Brahma is also said to have hatched from the golden cosmic egg that floated on primal waters. Earlier we described another popular creation myth in which Brahma emerges from a lotus sprouting from the navel of Vishnu. Originally considered the creator of the universe, Brahma was downgraded to just an agent of creation when other members of the triad gained supremacy. In fact Shiva or Vishnu or Devi is said to be the ultimate originator of the universe. Brahma is just the creator of our solar system.

Brahma, the creator god

BRAHMA – THE CREATOR GOD

Ever since he emerged from a lotus, Brahma's association with the flower is widely celebrated. Artists often have depicted him standing or sitting on a lotus with his four characteristic heads facing the four quarters of the world. Some Hindus regard this as symbolic of the four Vedas, whereas others stretch the significance to include the four yugas (described later) and the four *varnas* (castes). Brahma's face is often depicted with a hoary beard, for he is considered the god of wisdom. He has four arms, which hold different objects, including a water pot, a rosary, and a book. His vehicle is the swan, which represents spiritual transcendence and is said to have the power to separate water from milk—a bit later we'll find out if this is true. Sometimes Brahma is shown riding in a chariot drawn by seven swans.

Brahma originally had only one head. He acquired four more, but Shiva chopped one off. The story goes back to the time when Brahma created a female partner from his own substance. Known as Shatarupa,[6] or "thousand forms," the young woman was so attractive that Brahma became enamored with his own creation. When she noticed that Brahma was looking at her, she became embarrassed and moved away to avoid his gaze. As she moved to the right, then to the left, and later behind him, a new head sprang from Brahma to gaze in each direction. Finally she rose upward to the sky. A fifth head promptly appeared in that direction, followed Shatarupa, and united with her. An enraged Shiva is said to have used the thumbnail of his left hand to cut off Brahma's fifth head. Although ancient texts mention many motives for the loss of the Brahma's fifth head, one reason was punishment for committing incest with his daughter.

Troubling life events can trigger a downward spiral. This act of wantonness caused Brahma to lose his popularity. Furthermore, Brahma is considered a soft god and often seen as a liability because of his predilection for granting boons. He is almost always involved in heavenly conflicts and is easily placated. Brahma has often rewarded gods and demons for

---

[6] Shatarupa is also known variously as Vac, Gayatri, Saraswati, and Brahmani.

austerities they undertook by bestowing on them what is sometimes called the "boon of conditional immortality." Although his boons did not grant complete immortality, they always caused a great deal of concern for the gods. Eventually either Vishnu or Shiva uses the loophole in Brahma's boon to defeat the demon and restore the world to its rightful order.

Along with his consort Saraswati, Brahma resides in Mount Meru, the mythical abode of the gods. While Brahma represents the Vedas, Saraswati epitomizes their spirit and meaning. Despite the strong association of Brahma with the Vedas, he is not mentioned in the Vedas directly, for Brahma is known by other names like Prajapati and Hiranyagarbha. Other names include Pitamaha (the patriarch), Kanja (born in water), and Nabhija (born from the navel). Although the ubiquitous Narayana refers to Vishnu, it was originally a moniker of Brahma and meant "the one who dwells in the primal waters."

Today Brahma is invoked in Hindu rituals and resides in almost every temple of Shiva or Vishnu, usually in the northern wall. However, despite being an important member of the Trimurti, only a few temples have Brahma as the chief deity. The famous ones include the Brahma temple at Pushkar, Rajasthan; the Erawan Shrine of Bangkok (Thailand); and the Brahma temple at Tirunavaya, Kerala. Temples dedicated to Brahma can also be found in the temple compound of Prambanan, located in Java, Indonesia, and within the complexes of Angkor Wat, Cambodia.

Although Brahma is not as popular as Shiva or Vishnu today, scholars believe that the Brahma cult became predominant in the late Vedic period. The story of the boar that raised the earth from beneath the water was originally a tale associated with Brahma. Furthermore, some of the early avatars of Vishnu, such as the tortoise and fish avatars, were initially attributed to Brahma. The Brahma temple at Pushkar was the starting point for pilgrimages even from the times of the epics. But Brahma was not as glamorous as Shiva or Vishnu. He did not have any tales of manifestations or avatars like Rama or Krishna. Furthermore, creativity has its own land mines. As a creator god, Brahma is not the favorite deity of a soul crying out for moksha (escape from the cycle of reincarnation).

A large statue of Brahma at the Wat Saman
Rattanaram Temple in Chachoengsao, Thailand

The evolution of the concept of Shakti also contributed to his decline. The idea of creation was usurped by Shakti, for those who subscribe to this belief consider the consorts of Shiva and Vishnu responsible for their power, or Shakti. Because creation proceeds from the union of the god and his Shakti, Brahma's career prospects as a creator god took a turn for the worse. As a result, the Brahma cult gradually declined in popularity. Consequently, as the Shiva and Vishnu cults gained strength, their devotees borrowed the early tales of Brahma and applied them to their heroes.

Let's now answer the question posed at the beginning: Can a swan separate milk and water? The answer is no. The ability to separate milk from water is symbolic of the power to discriminate between righteousness and evil. Hindu mythology bestows this power on the swan. Called *hamsa* in most Indian languages, the swan is revered in Hinduism and has the status of a saint. A person of exceptional spiritual capability is often called Paramahamsa,[7] or supreme swan. Among them are spiritual teachers like Ramakrishna Paramahamsa and Paramahamsa Yogananda. As the mount of both Brahma and Saraswati, the swan is a symbol of prudence. For Brahma, however, prudence took a hit during Puranic times, when he was condemned for his incestuous relationship with his own creation.

> *Take the first a out of Abraham and put it at the end.*
> *You get Brahama. There's the ancient connection right there.*
>
> —ASHWIN SANGHI, 1969-

> *[As] Vishnu sleeps in the cosmic ocean, the lotus of the universe grows from his navel. On there sits Brahma the creator. Brahma opens his eyes, a world comes into being, governed by an Indra. [Brahma] closes his eyes, the world goes out of being. Opens his eyes, the world comes into being; closes his eyes ... And the life of a Brahma is 432,000 years [sic], and he dies. The lotus goes back, another lotus, another Brahma. And then think of the galaxies beyond galaxies in infinite space; each a lotus with the Brahma sitting on it, opening his eyes, closing his eyes with Indras. There may be wise men in your court who would volunteer to count the drops of water in the oceans of the world, or the grains of sand on the beaches, but no one would count those Brahmas, let alone those Indras.*
>
> —JOSEPH CAMPBELL, 1904-1987

---

[7] Hamsa is sometimes spelled as hansa. Similarly, Paramahamsa is also occasionally spelled as Paramahansa.

3

A Day of Brahma

A lot of things can happen in a day, particularly in a cosmic day, where time is measured not by the 24-hour clock but by the cosmic unit of time called *kalpa*, defined as a day of Brahma. According to Hindu mythology, Brahma is busy creating the world during the day, but when he is sleeping at night, the three worlds—the heavens, middle earth, and the nether regions—are reduced to *pralaya*, or dissolution. Every being that has not obtained liberation is judged and has to be prepared for rebirth when Brahma wakes up the next day. The alternating cycles of day and night continue until Brahma reaches the hundredth year of his life when the final dissolution of the universe—called *maha-pralaya*—begins with the cosmic shake dance of Shiva. Not only the three worlds but the *devas* (demigods), *asuras* (demons), *rishis* (Hindu sages), and just about everything in the world is dissolved, including Brahma himself. This is followed by one hundred years of inactivity, after which another Brahma is born and a new cycle begins.

What exactly is the duration of a *kalpa* and how does it correlate with our 24-hour day? To answer this question, let us go back to basics. In Hinduism time is calculated in yugas, of which there are four, as set out in the table that follows.

	Hindu Time Cycles	Years
1	Satya/Krita Yuga	1,728, 000 years (4 x Kali Yuga)
2	Treta Yuga	1,296,000 years (3 x Kali Yuga)
3	Dvapara Yuga	864,000 years (2 x Kali Yuga)
4	Kali Yuga	432,000 years
	Total (maha-yuga)	**4,320,000 years**

One complete cycle that involves the four yugas is called a *maha-yuga* (sometimes called *chatur-yuga*), a span of 4,320,000 years. Thus a *maha-yuga* starts with the longest, Satya Yuga, followed by Treta and Dvapara, and finally Kali. Each age witnesses a decline in dharma (virtue) from the previous age. It is said that dharma initially stands on four legs like a table with full support at all points, but by the second age it wobbles on three, followed by two in the next age, and finally dangles on one in Kali Yuga. Hindus believe we are living in Kali Yuga today and that this cycle started about 5,000 years ago.[8]

A thousand *maha-yugas* is called a *kalpa*; therefore a *kalpa*—an ordinary day of Brahma—is 4.32 billion human years. According to the Hindu tradition, time moves in these great cycles, yuga after yuga, *kalpa* after *kalpa*, eternally. The lifetime of Brahma is one hundred years; each year has 360 days and 360 nights (which are counted separately).

Lifetime of Brahma =
100 x 360 x 2 x 4.32 billion = 311.04 trillion human years[9]

What happens after Brahma's death? Hindus believe the universe undergoes a cyclical period of inactivity for another hundred years before the advent of a new Brahma. The destruction of the universe begins in

---

[8] The Kali Yuga supposedly began around 3102 BCE.
[9] A day of Brahma is also 2.16 billion days in the lunar calendar.

events known as *pralaya*, which refers to the cataclysm caused by fire or water or any other calamity that results in the dissolution of the world. After the world is destroyed, it lies in a state of rest. The *pralaya* is not, however, confined to the aftermath of Brahma's death. It occurs in every major Hindu time cycle. Although popularly referred to as a night of Brahma, *pralaya* also follows a *maha-yuga* or a *manvantara*.

This brings us to the concept of *manvantara*. Each day of Brahma—or *kalpa*—is further divided into 14 *manvantaras*, each comprising 306.72 million days, or about 71 *maha-yugas*. A Manu presides over each *manvantara* as the father of the human race and perishes during the *pralaya* at the end of the *manvantara*. There are exceptions, of course. For instance, the sage Markandeya relates in the Mahabharata how a measly fish saved the current Manu during the last *pralaya*—a story which we describe in the next chapter.

Thus there are 14 Manus in each day of Brahma, and the division of time is called a *manvantara* in honor of Manu. The present age is considered the seventh Manu cycle. According to mythical astronomy, Brahma has just completed his 50th year, and we are approaching noon on the first day of his sixth decade.[10] A back-of-the-envelope calculation reveals that the world has thus far seen 252,000 Manus in addition to the seven Manus created so far today.[11] The *manvantaras* are not just about the lives and times of Manus. With the coming of a new Manu, the title of Indra passes to the most deserving of the *devas*, and along with it new appointments to the positions of the seven *rishis* are also made. Thus Manu and Indra are also administrative positions, with Manu as the king on earth and Indra the king of heaven.

---

[10] To be precise, we are in the seventh *manvantara* and currently in Kali Yuga of the twenty-eighth *maha-yuga*. According to Hindu traditions, the present Kali Yuga started in 3102 BCE (based on the epics), and 5,120 years have passed as of 2018.

[11] That is, 14 x 360 x 50 = 252,000 Manus from the previous 50 Brahma years plus seven for today = 252,007 Manus.

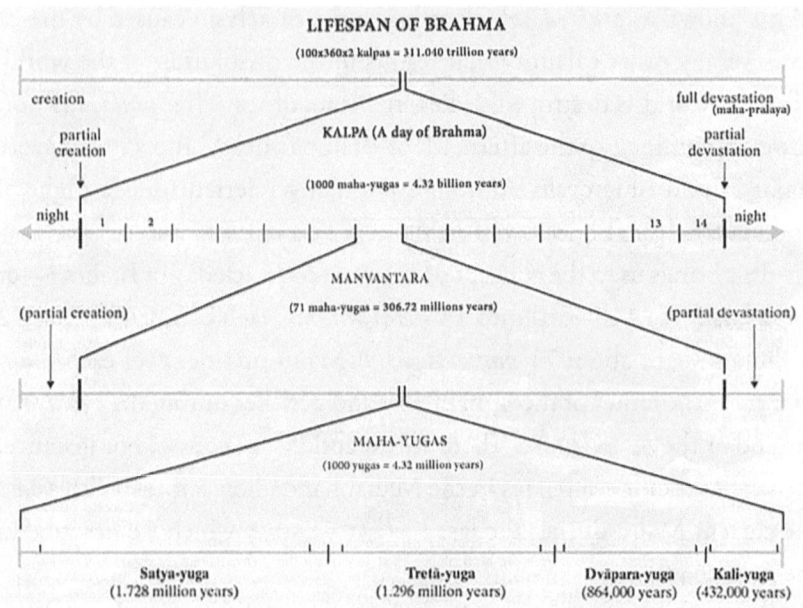

Lifetime of Brahma in Hindu time periods

As you can see, the key roles and portfolios are recycled at varying times in Hinduism. Whereas Brahma is recycled every one hundred Brahma years, Indra and the seven sages are replaced over *manvantaras*. But the drama and plots and subplots of the gods and divine beings are not recycled and become unique to each *manvantara*. Many creation myths or multiple parenthoods exist in Hinduism because they sometimes originated during past *manvantaras*. For instance, the popular creation myth of the churning of the ocean occurred in the previous *manvantara*, or when the sixth Manu was presiding over earth.

Thus a day of Brahma is packed with a lot of events and drama. Compared with the time cycles of Hinduism, our human life span seems short and insignificant. The underlying message is that we are just ripples that arise at a point in time on the grand cosmic ocean, only to vanish over time, but those ripples may in turn lead to another ripple or even a tsunami, for everything in the Hindu world is recycled, including our souls.

A DAY OF BRAHMA

Before we turn to the next chapter, please be reminded this is the only math we'll be doing in this book. Period. There is no Brahma's Theory of Relativity or Vishwakarma's Laws of Motion to keep us engaged further. If you are keen for a mathematical challenge, try working out the lifetimes of Vishnu and Shiva.

> *The Hindu religion is the only one of the world's great faiths dedicated to the idea that the Cosmos itself undergoes an immense, indeed an infinite, number of deaths and rebirths. It is the only religion in which the time scales correspond to those of modern scientific cosmology. Its cycles run from our ordinary day and night to a day and night of Brahma, 8.64 billion years long. Longer than the age of the Earth or the Sun and about half the time since the Big Bang. And there are much longer time scales still.*
>
> —CARL SAGAN, 1934-1996

4

Manu and the Flood Myth

Kindness is the language which the deaf can hear and the blind can see.

—MARK TWAIN, 1835-1910

"No act of kindness, no matter how small, is ever wasted," says an Aesopian proverb. History is chockfull of stories of simple acts that have turned into life-changing, history-making occasions. The story of Manu is one such tale about a small act of kindness that allowed him to survive the Great Deluge.[12]

Manu, the son of the sun god Surya, was washing his hands in a river one morning when a small fish swam into them. The fish pleaded with Manu to take it home because it feared the bigger fish in the river would devour it. Manu agreed and kept the fish in a bowl of water. The fish soon grew too large for the bowl. Manu transferred the fish to a small

---

[12] The story of Krishna and Kuchela is another such tale which is described in book 4 of this series.

pond. When it outgrew the pond, he released the fish into the sea. In return for his kindness the fish warned him of an imminent flood and advised him to build a ship to save himself. True to the fish's words, clouds began to fill up the sky and the torrential rains began to flood the entire landmass. Manu rushed into his ship and took shelter inside, but the ship was drifting about in the raging waters. The fish suddenly reappeared with a horn on its head. With a rope from the ship tied to its horn, the fish towed Manu to the safety of a nearby mountain. The waters swept away everything in its course, and Manu was saved.

Vishnu emerging from Matsya, 19th century painting (artist unknown)

The story doesn't end there. When the waters subsided, Manu repopulated the world, for he had taken a pair of each living species and the Seven Rishis (sages) with him on the ship, just as the fish had instructed.

Let us pause for a moment to talk about Manu. Hindus have many Manus. They regard Manu as an administrative position that is filled at the start of every *manvantara*. As we discussed in a previous chapter, a day of Brahma, or *kalpa*,[13] can be divided into 14 *manvantaras*. A specific Manu, created by Brahma, rules during each *manvantara* (literally, the life span of Manu). That is why Manu is called the father of the human race—all human beings can trace their ancestry to Manu. Indeed *Manu* is the root of both the Sanskrit Manushya (human being) and the English word *man*. In the Vedas, however, Manu appears as the one who performs

---

[13] A *kalpa* is 4.32 billion human years, whereas a *manvantara* is 306.72 million human years.

the first sacrifice. He is also known as the first king. Most rulers of medieval India traced their ancestry to him.

If Manu is the first man and also the flood survivor, then who is he—Adam or Noah? To answer that question, remember that we are living in the seventh *manvantara* and our Manu is Vaivasvata Manu, the one who survived the flood. Vaivasvata Manu is considered the counterpart of Noah. The Manu of the first *manvantara*, called Swayambhuva Manu, is regarded as the first man and the Indian counterpart of Adam. Swayambhuva Manu is believed to have written the Manusmriti, a Hindu law book often seen as overly protective of women. Hindu scriptures state that Swayambhuva Manu emerged from Brahma's body when Brahma was exhausted after creating the *devas*, *asuras*, sages, and others. At the same time Brahma formed a feminine principal called Shatarupa. (Yes, the same Shatarupa with whom Brahma became enchanted and which led to the loss of his fifth head.) Under Brahma's orders Swayambhuva Manu and Shatarupa established their dominion on earth. Human beings are the descendants of Swayambhuva Manu.[14] Brahma also created the Saptarishis, or seven sages. Because the sages were born from the mind of Brahma, they are known as mind-born sons, or *manasaputras*.

The flood myth of Manu has its parallel in the biblical account of Noah, when God saves Noah from the flood by instructing him to build an ark. While the destruction of the world in the Hebrew Bible is divine punishment, the Hindu myth treats it as part of a natural order of cosmic activity in which the world undergoes *pralaya* after the passing of each *manvantara*. In both accounts, however, divine intervention saves humanity from total destruction. The fish in the Hindu myth is actually Vishnu in his first avatar, which is known as the Matsya avatar.[15]

The ancient flood myth has found its way into other civilizations of the world. Accounts of a great deluge appear in ancient Zoroastrian

---

[14] Some scholars maintain that each Manu is considered the father of the human race of his respective *manvantara*.

[15] We will discuss the Matsya avatar in book 3 of this series.

mythology and Sumerian tablets. Earlier scholars thought the Sumerian version of the myth, which dates to 1750 BCE, was the oldest. However, with the re-dating of Vedic texts, the Hindu myth, first recorded in the Shatapatha Brahmana, has emerged as the most ancient version of this famous story.

❄ ❄ ❄

5

Trimurti – The Hindu Triad

The Trimurti is a well-established Hindu concept by which the three gods—Brahma the creator, Vishnu the preserver, and Shiva the destroyer—personify the cosmic functions of creation, maintenance, and destruction. The three gods are often addressed as Brahma-Vishnu-Shiva and are known as the Hindu triad or the Great Trinity. The Trimurti is sometimes represented by the acronym GOD—which stands for Generator (Brahma), Operator (Vishnu), and Destroyer (Shiva).

The three deities are regarded as the manifestation of Absolute Reality, or Brahman, and they occupy a unique position in the Hindu pantheon. Unlike other deities, they are not subject to the doctrine of transmigration of souls (*samsara*) and are considered superior to all other forms of beings. In this context they are sometimes called *mahadevas*, or great gods.

Most scholars concur that the emergence of the Trimurti was an attempt to reconcile the major Hindu deities of the time as one universal god and to foster unity and harmony among devotees. Before the Trimurti emerged, Hindus made many attempts to unify their various traditions but achieved little success. The concept of a divine triad had its roots in the early Hindu solar cults, which worshipped the sun as the creator for its fertilizing warmth, the preserver for its revealing light, and the destroyer for its burning rays. The early Vedic deities of Varuna, Mitra, and Aryaman formed the original triad. Varuna and Mitra are still remembered today, but Aryaman lost his significance and is mostly invoked today as a witness to Hindu rituals. During Rigvedic times (1500–500 BCE) the original triad was replaced with Vayu, Agni, and Surya. Later Vayu gave way to Indra because of Indra's popularity.

By the time the epics were composed, the nature gods of the Vedic period had fallen out of favor, and the gods Shiva and Vishnu had ascended to the top of the Hindu pantheon. No attempt was made to identify a triad during the epic period, but the combined form of Vishnu

Sculpture of Trimurti at Elephanta Caves, Mumbai, India

and Shiva, called Harihara, gained significance and was worshipped as a form of the Absolute Reality. It was not until the arrival of the Puranas that the Trimurti, as we know them today, became accepted as standard doctrine. One of the earliest images of Trimurti can be found at one of the many caves on Elephanta,[16] an island near Mumbai, India. Carved between the fifth and eighth centuries CE, this giant statue depicts Shiva manifesting all three aspects of the Trimurti—an image that the French art historian Rene Grousset (1885–1952) described as "the greatest representation of the pantheistic god created by the hands of man."

Which is the most important god in the Trimurti? According to the theory of Brahmanism, no one deity should take precedence over the other two in the triad. That is, all are equal and each may represent Brahman. The fifth-century poet Kalidasa, widely regarded as one of India's preeminent Sanskrit poets, says:

> *In those three persons the one God was shown*
> *Each first in place, each last – not one alone*
> *Of Brahma, Vishnu, Shiva, each may be*
> *First, second, third, among the blessed Three.*

Although various sects of Hinduism accepted the oneness of the Trimurti, the equality of the three gods was lost in later times. While Brahma came to be worshipped less, the other two gained honor and importance. The different sects in Hinduism often conceived the Trimurti as the three manifestations of their own sectarian god. For instance, Vaishnavas believe Vishnu alone to be the supreme god with Shiva as subordinate. For Shaivites, or Shiva worshippers, Trimurti is a form of Shiva himself, as reflected in the 20-foot image of Trimurti at Elephanta. They believe Brahma and Vishnu are different forms of Shiva. Surya is the supreme god of the Saura sect. Devi worshippers, in contrast, believe Trimurti originated from Adi Parashakti (primordial force).[17] The concept

---

[16] Elephanta is a UNESCO World Heritage site.

[17] Book 6 in this series explores goddess worship in detail.

of Trimurti, however, is most strongly held by Smartism, a contemporary denomination of Hinduism based on the principles of Advaita Vedanta, a school of Hindu religious practice. Instead of emphasizing the three forms of divinity, Smartas focus on five forms of god that correspond to the following deities: Ganesha, Vishnu, Shiva, Devi, and Surya. The notable omission is Brahma. Shakti worshipers, on the other hand, believe the three deities emerge from Mother Goddess and are merely aspects of her nature. It's fair to say that using the concept of Trimurti to unify various sects of Hinduism achieved only limited success.

The Trimurti of Hinduism finds its parallel in the Christian Trinity, although they have little in common. In the Trinity, god exists as a unity of three people: Father, Son, and Holy Spirit. The Trimurti, however, is a manifestation of the Supreme Spirit (Brahman) in three forms: Brahma, Vishnu, and Shiva. These deities have attained the highest states possible, short of absorption into Brahman. A key distinction between the two triads is that the Hindu Trimurti can be subordinated or dropped in rank. In that sense all lesser divinities, such as Indra, Agni, Surya, and others, are subordinate aspects of the one god. Thus the Supreme God, or Brahman, can be reached through the Brahma-Vishnu-Shiva combo, through any one god of the triad, or through any of the innumerable gods, goddesses, or saints. Although many Hindus center their worship on Vishnu, others worship Shiva, Durga, Surya, Mata Amritanandamayi, or even lesser-known figures. While most Hindu sects tend to favor one god of the Trimurti, others honor deities that are not even members of the triad. In short, the Trimurti was an artificial device and never had any real influence on the religion.

6

Brahman – The Ultimate Reality

As the most powerful and supreme god of the Hindus, Brahman is a mysterious spirit that pervades the cosmos. No one knows what he looks like, for he is not a man or a woman—not even creature. He is not worshipped, for no temples are dedicated to him. People regularly confuse him with Brahma and Brahmin. When Brahman takes on the form of a handsome young man and plays the flute, he becomes the cynosure of all eyes and the darling of his disciples. Hordes of women are attracted to him. Devotees chant mantras and *shlokas* (poetry) for him, joyfully make sacrifices for him, and even dedicate their entire life to serving him. But the handsome young man, Krishna, is only one of Brahman's many forms.

The English language uses the word *godhead* to describe the essence of god. For most Christians the three separate people—Father, Son, and Holy Spirit—make up the godhead. Although the Semitic[18] religions perceive god as male, Hindus take the idea to a higher level and conceive the deity as gender neutral. The Supreme Being, otherwise known as Brahman, is without gender or attributes. Brahman is that changeless,

---

[18] The three main Semitic religions are Judaism, Christianity, and Islam.

formless, underlying reality that pervades, creates, and transcends everything—including our world and each one of us. The world is in a constant state of change, but Brahman is never changing. If Brahman is the infinite ocean, we are ripples created at a point in time and perish with the passage of time.

Hindus call the genderless, eternal, infinite, and changeless form of Brahman as Nirguna Brahman. This form of the Brahman cannot assume a personality, since attaching even a well-meaning personality can itself become a limitation. Hindus also use expressions like Absolute Reality, Ultimate Reality, Consciousness, and Infinite Bliss to describe Nirguna Brahman. Although Brahman cannot be known, it can be experienced at the highest state of consciousness. The scriptures state that the most one can say about Brahman is *sat-chid-ananda,* meaning "existence-consciousness-bliss."

The mind has difficulty visualizing Nirguna Brahman because the human mind is capable of thinking only in human terms. So we resort to metaphors, and these metaphors unwittingly give human attributes to Nirguna Brahman. The impersonal Brahman then acquires a human-like personality called Saguna Brahman. Thus Saguna Brahman, or Brahman with human attributes, was born to help devotees focus their minds and serve the lord. For instance, Shiva is the embodiment of renunciation and divine consciousness. As the protector Vishnu is the divine principle that permeates the entire universe. Rama is not just the ideal man; he's the personification of all virtues. The flute-wielding Krishna, mentioned at the beginning of this chapter, represents the highest ideal of divine love. Yet Shiva and Vishnu and Rama and Krishna are different forms of Saguna Brahman and identify with the supreme spirit, Nirguna Brahman.

More than a hundred hymns in the Vedas refer to Brahman. In the early Vedic period Prajapati was the Supreme Being, and *Brahman* referred to the power associated with sounds, words, and rituals. Brahman was the secret behind Vedic chants and sacrifices. The current meaning of Brahman was conceived during the time of the Upanishads, and it became one of the important concepts of Hinduism. The central teachings of

Hinduism, such as the concepts of karma (action), samsara (reincarnation), moksha (liberation), and atman (soul), are also found in the Upanishads.

Brahman is often confused with *Brahmin*. The latter refers to the caste or a member of the caste and sometimes is spelled *Brahman*, especially in older texts. Brahman is also confused with the creator god Brahma, who is just one aspect of the all-prevailing Brahman.

> *Brahman is beyond mind and speech, beyond concentration and meditation, beyond the knower, the known and knowledge, beyond even the conception of the real and unreal. In short, it is beyond all relativity.*
>
> —RAMAKRISHNA PARAMAHAMSA, 1836-1886

7

The Churning of the Milky Ocean

For you and me the word *immortality* conjures notions of bliss and freedom from death. In Hindu mythology, however, immortality means not just longevity but supremacy in the ongoing battle between the gods and demons. The churning of the milky ocean is a pivotal event in Hindu mythology and is the quest for *amrita*, the elixir of immortality. Such is its significance that the story appears in many texts, including the Bhagavata Purana, the Mahabharata, and the Vishnu Purana. Often called *samudra manthan*, it is the story of the genesis of many goddesses and the discovery of a slew of treasures and supernatural animals. Although the story is essentially a Vaishnava myth, the milky ocean has a special significance for the 700 million Vaishnavas, who speak in glowing terms of their lord's Ananda Sayana. This is the famous position in which Vishnu sleeps blissfully on an ocean of milk before the creation of the universe. The position is depicted on the stone walls of many temples and is often mentioned in devotional songs.

The origin of the story traces to the Vedic hero Indra, who was once riding a wild elephant when he bumped into the sage Durvasa. The sage was pleased to meet Indra and presented him with a garland of fragrant

THE ASCENT OF VISHNU AND THE FALL OF BRAHMA

Vishnu in Ananda Sayana (watercolor ca. 1870)

flowers that Shiva had given to Durvasa. As lord of the three worlds, Indra graciously accepted the garland but casually placed it on the trunk of the elephant. The animal threw it to the ground and trampled it with its feet. Durvasa, who was known for his extremely short fuse, was insulted by this, even though the slight was accidental. He immediately put a curse on Indra, that he would lose his power over the three worlds.

The curses of sages are never known to miss their mark. Soon thereafter the demons defeated the gods and gained control of the universe. The powerless gods went to Vishnu, who analyzed the situation with a seriousness usually reserved for the Middle-East crisis talks. He advised the gods that the secret to permanent power is to obtain *amrita* by churning the ocean. This is a massive task, Vishnu warned, and the weakened gods would need assistance from their arch enemies, the demons. The gods took Vishnu's advice and struck an alliance with the demons to jointly churn the ocean for *amrita* and share it.

Thus the quest for *amrita* began with the agreement to partake of both the burden and the rewards. As Vishnu had warned, the task was an elaborate one. First they had to throw herbs into the clear waters. Then they had to tear out Mount Mandara, a spur of Mount Meru, and use it as a churning rod. The giant snake Vasuki, which adorns Shiva's neck, became the churning rope. The gods took its tail, while the *asuras* grabbed Vasuki's head with its fiery breath. The gods and demons pulled back and forth alternately, causing the mountain to rotate like an agitator washing machine in its wash cycle, and the rotation churned the ocean. The stirring motion, however, slowly caused the mountain to sink. Vishnu came to their assistance as his turtle avatar by providing support for the

The churning of the milky ocean, 19th century painting by Raja Ravi Varma

mountain from below. He simultaneously took an invisible form to hold the mountain steady at the top.

As the churning progressed for a thousand years, many amazing things rose to the surface from the depths of the ocean. They included treasures, supernatural animals, and even goddesses. Among the treasures were Kaustubha, the jewel worn by Vishnu, and the Parijata tree, which would later become the envy of one of Krishna's wife. Born of this action was Lakshmi, the goddess of fortune and the consort of Vishnu; the *apsaras* Rambha and Menaka; and Varuni, the goddess of wine and Varuna's consort. The supernatural animals that came out of the churning ocean included the seven-headed horse Uchchaihsravas; the wish-granting cow Kamadhenu; and the elephant Airavata, which later became the favorite mount of Indra.

Finally Dhanavantari, the physician of the gods, emerged holding the pot of *amrita* in his hands. Both the gods and demons were overjoyed, but before they could receive the nectar, a poison called Halahala came out and terrified the deities. The poison was so virulent that it had the power

Bas-relief of the churning of the milky ocean, Angkor Wat temple, Cambodia

to destroy the entire world. Shiva saved the world by swallowing the poison, but Parvati was alarmed by her husband's act and prevented him from swallowing it by holding his throat with her hands. This act earned Shiva the moniker Neelakanta, which means "the blue-throated one."

When the *amrita* finally appeared, there was no orderly line of heavenly deities standing with cups in their hands. Rather a mad scramble ensued. To the gods' chagrin, the demons grabbed the pot from Dhanavantari and made a run for it. They had violated the original agreement to share it equally, so the gods appealed to Vishnu, who decided that because of their deceit the demons did not deserve the *amrita*. In an attempt to stop the rampaging demons, Vishnu turned into his Mohini avatar and reappeared as a beautiful and enchanting damsel. The sudden appearance of a beautiful woman startled the demons. At first they looked at her with distrust, but slowly they became enthralled by her intoxicating beauty. The demons were convinced that the infinite power they would gain from drinking the *amrita* would protect them from any countermeasure the gods might take. Mohini confided in the *asuras* that she was lonely and looking for companionship. All the demons raised their hands at once to alleviate her loneliness, but soon they realized only one would be able to befriend her. With so many demons to choose from, Mohini asked them to close their eyes. She said she would marry the one who opened them last.

While the demons closed their eyes and dreamed about possessing the most beautiful woman, Mohini started to distribute the *amrita* among the gods. All the gods drank it, but not all demons were fooled by Mohini. The *asura* Rahuketu disguised himself as a god and drank some nectar. The sun and moon gods, who were sitting next to the demon, noticed the imposter and informed Mohini. Before Rahuketu could swallow the nectar, Mohini turned into his real form and flung the divine discus, Sudarshana Chakra, at the demon's throat, severing his head from his body. But because the nectar had entered his throat, Rahuketu survived and later became two planets, Rahu the head and Ketu the torso. According to legend, Rahu and Ketu became lifelong enemies of the sun and moon. The eclipse is now said to occur when these demons swallow the sun and moon to exact their revenge.

The thousand years of churning took its toll on Vasuki as it became the longest snake in mythology. When the demons woke up from their dreams, they realized they had been tricked into giving up *amrita*. Enraged, the demons attacked at once, but the gods, fortified by the divine drink, were able to repel them and established dominion over the three worlds.

The churning of the milky ocean was a massive collaboration project undertaken by many participants. In the end the gods became victorious and were awarded with immortality. The *asuras* had to settle for the crumbs of victory, and their stories became immortal.

> *I'm not a Republican, but I was one once—when I was 7 years old. Not my fault. The symbol of the Republican Party is an elephant, I'm a Hindu—I was confused.*
>
> –HARI KONDABOLU, 1982-

8

Who Among the Gods is the Greatest?

Now tell me this: In Hinduism the supreme gods—Brahma, Vishnu, and Shiva—constitute the Trimurti, but which is the most revered? According to the theory of Brahmanism, no deity should take precedence over the others, for all are equal, right? Well, that's theory, but mythology is a different beast. It defies gravity and does not follow any rules or theory. If you were to ask who the greatest god is, the answer depends on whom you are asking. For a Vaishnava the greatest is undoubtedly Vishnu. For a Shaivite the response can only be Shiva. Unfortunately Brahma does not have a large following to vouch his superiority. Yet Brahma once considered himself the most revered, as the following myth reveals.

Once Vishnu and Brahma were overcome with pride and got caught up in a dispute about which of them was more venerable. Because the argument became so heated and neither was willing to concede, they sought Shiva's intervention. Suddenly a fiery pillar of light as luminous as a thousand cosmic fires appeared before them. Both gods were dumbfounded by the sight and wondered where it came from. To find the source Vishnu took the form a colossal boar and followed the column downward. Meanwhile Brahma turned into a swift-moving swan and traveled upward along the column. The search lasted for a thousand years, but neither could reach the end. Exhausted, they abandoned the search and returned to ground zero, smaller than their heavenly stature.

Sculpture of Trimurti (l-r Brahma, Vishnu, and Shiva), Ellora caves

When Brahma and Vishnu met again under friendlier circumstances, Shiva appeared before them. Upon seeing Shiva, Vishnu realized that the column of light had been Shiva's *linga*, his universal symbol. Vishnu at once acknowledged that Shiva was the greatest and most venerable of the gods. Brahma, however, falsely claimed that he had reached the summit of the *linga*, thus proving his superiority. Because Brahma was lying, Shiva decided that Brahma should no longer serve as a role model. He put a curse on Brahma that mortals would never worship him or dedicate temples to him.

This tale illustrates the importance of power in Hindu mythology, where demons often become a danger to the gods not for their crimes, but for their power. While the Greek ideal is beauty and the Christian quintessence is love, the Hindu ideal is mostly about power, with the exception of Krishna's love themes—something we'll explore in book 4 of this series. But the Linga of Light was a Shaiva myth. A Vaishnava version of the same myth ends by establishing the supremacy of Vishnu. In this version Brahma again fibs about reaching the pinnacle, while Vishnu confesses he was unsuccessful in finding the base. On hearing this Shiva cuts off one of Brahma's heads and crowns Vishnu as the greatest of the Trimurti for speaking the truth.

> *The glorious Vishnu is the sole refuge of mortals. He is Infinite Light, Love and Wisdom. He resides in the hearts of all beings. His Grace is invincible. He is in all. He is the Highest Truth. He is Infinite Bliss. He is the Protector. He is the Preserver. He is the Savior.*
>
> —SWAMI SIVANANDA, 1887-1963

9

Vishnu – The Preserver God

"I am the greatest! I'm the greatest thing that ever lived," declared a 22-year old kid, way back in the 1960s. No one took him seriously then, but within a few years this American boxer, who went by the name of Muhammad Ali, became one of the unforgettable people in sports. Bluster, however, is not unique to sport but a phenomenon present in many aspects of life. Everyone looks up to superstars like Ali or Sachin Tendulkar, one of the best cricketers ever, for hero worship is an intrinsic part of human nature. In Hinduism an oft-repeated question is who among the higher gods is the greatest. It seems every major Hindu denomination has laid its claim to this title, a claim often validated by a slew of ancient myths.

Earlier we discussed the old Shaiva myth that held Shiva superior to both Brahma and Vishnu. Yet another myth along the same lines revolves around Saptarishi Bhrigu, who was entrusted with the task of ascertaining the greatest god by his fellow sages. Initially Bhrigu thought about recusing himself from conducting the test because Brahma was Bhrigu's father. Bhrigu nevertheless acceded to their request. Years of austerities and penance in the forest had taught him to be fair and unbiased in his decisions. Instead of testing the gods with superhuman tasks like chasing the end of an infinite light beam or circling the world in the fastest time, Bhrigu focused on a certain aspect of behavior: How do the gods react to provocation? Will the gods maintain their godly nature? Or will their animal instincts come into play? (Disclosure: Bhrigu himself is not in the hall of fame for his patience.)

To put this test in to action, Bhrigu went to Mount Meru, the heaven of Brahma, and entered his court. Showing no warmth or affection, he deliberately failed to treat his father with the customary respect and to abide by protocol. As the creator of our universe, Brahma was offended by this slight and scowled at Bhrigu. Nevertheless Brahma was able to assuage his anger in time and avert a potential tragedy. Bhrigu apologized to Brahma and headed to Kailash, the abode of Shiva, where Shiva embraced him warmly like a brother. When Bhrigu did not respond to his hospitality, Shiva became enraged and seized his trident. Parvati interceded and fell at Shiva's feet, begging him to spare Bhrigu's life. Bhrigu wondered what would have happened if Parvati had not intervened.

The sage went next to Vaikuntha, the abode of Vishnu, where he found him in blissful slumber with Lakshmi stroking his feet. Bhrigu climbed onto the cot of the sleeping deity and jumped on Vishnu's chest despite protests from Lakshmi. Vishnu rose at once and, on seeing the sage, apologized for not greeting him on his arrival. Vishnu then asked whether Bhrigu had hurt his feet. Without waiting for a reply, Vishnu bent down and massaged his feet, only to realize that he has passed the test with flying colors. Bhrigu was overwhelmed by this gesture and returned to his colleagues to proclaim that Vishnu was indeed the greatest of the gods. No god at his level could match his tolerance and generosity.

So was Vishnu the greatest of them all? It should be pointed out that diplomacy and equanimity are requirements for Vishnu's role as preserver of the universe, just as impulsiveness serves Shiva well in his role as the destroyer. So, strictly speaking, Bhrigu was testing a quality that was a prerequisite for the preserver role. Furthermore, the myth comes to us from the Bhagavata Purana, a book sacred to the Vaishnavas.

Giant statue of Vishnu in Bali, Indonesia

That said, although Shaivites may dispute his superiority, Vishnu is widely recognized as the most lovable member of the Trimurti. Courteous and considerate, he is full of forgiveness and tender thoughts for his devotees. So you have made mistakes in the past and not paid Vishnu his due respect? That's okay. Vishnu is the not the type who keeps a scorecard of petty issues and dwells on them. He is always looking after the welfare of gods and humans, is more forgiving than vindictive, and takes a long-term interest in his *bhaktas*. He is known to be extremely loyal to them and to anyone who thinks about him, as the story of Shishupala attests.

In his past life Shishupala was called Jaya and was the doorkeeper of Vishnu's abode at Vaikuntha. For his failure to carry out dharma on another occasion, Jaya was cursed to have three rebirths. In his third rebirth as Shishupala, he was born as the son of a local king. As a baby, he looked weird with three eyes and four hands. When his parents noticed the third eye, they were thrilled, convinced their little one was a manifestation of Shiva, but their hopes were dashed when the boy started braying like an ass. The parents tried to quietly abandon the baby, but a voice from above informed them that his deformity would disappear in the lap of a warrior. The voice also warned them that the same warrior eventually would destroy the child.

Vishnu, the preserver (bazaar art ca. 1940)

Although the advice provided little comfort for the parents, the king went on a spree of putting the child in the lap of every warrior in the hope of reversing the boy's abnormality. Finally the miracle happened as predicted while the child was in the lap of his uncle Krishna. Devoid of deformities, Shishupala grew into a formidable youth worthy of respect, but fate had foretold his destiny. Krishna killed him during the great horse sacrifice in the Mahabharata but not before Krishna abducted Rukmini, Shishupala's fiancée, and made her his wife. This was not the first time Shishupala was killed by an avatar of Vishnu. In his previous births as Hiranyakashipu and Ravana, Shishupala committed many atrocities and was slain by other avatars of Vishnu. Yet Vishnu was generous toward Shishupala after his death. Because Shishupala spent so many lifetimes focused solely on his hatred for Vishnu, he obtained liberation, which ended his cycle of rebirths.

The name Vishnu is derived from the Sanskrit root *vish*, meaning "to pervade." Thus Vishnu pervades everything and every being as the soul. By extension every human being is an abode of god. Vaishnavas believe creation and destruction are change agents, for preservation is the only reality. Vishnu did not, however, have a pervasive presence in the early texts of the Vedic period, for he is mentioned only 93 times in the Rigveda, and just six hymns are dedicated to him, whereas 289 are dedicated to Indra. As a minor solar deity in the Rigveda, Vishnu is considered a close friend of Indra and participated in drinking soma. He also accompanied Indra in his celebrated battle against the demon Vritra. The most famous mention of Vishnu, however, is in the famous three steps of Vishnu, as Trivikrama, by which he strode over the universe and is the basis of his Vamana avatar. During the late Vedic period Vishnu rose from obscurity to prominence and became popular with the advent of the bhakti movement and the coming of his avatars, particularly Rama and Krishna. A measure of Vishnu's popularity can be seen in the fact that he has more temples dedicated to him than any other god, including Shiva. Vishnu is the only god in the Trimurti who has retained his Vedic name.

THE ASCENT OF VISHNU AND THE FALL OF BRAHMA

Picture of Trivikrama in a temple in Bhaktapur, Nepal.
The exaggerated three strides of Vishnu are common in temple artwork

Vishnu has more than a thousand names, as listed in the Vishnu Sahasranama. The important ones are Hari, Narayana, and Vasudeva. In art the most famous of his representations is the Ananda Sayana, where Vishnu reclines serenely on the coils of a giant cobra called Ananda Shesha, which is floating on the ocean. This pose is the theme of hundreds of songs and the motif of many reliefs on temples. Vishnu is also represented in a standing position dressed in royal garments. At his neck is the miraculous jewel called the Kaustubha, and on his chest is a mark known as Srivatsa, where his consort, Lakshmi, is said to reside. His vehicle is Garuda, the sun eagle, taken from Surya. In paintings Vishnu is usually shown with a dark-blue complexion, a common feature of his incarnations as well. He is often portrayed as having four hands and holds items like a mace, a conch shell, and a lotus flower. In one hand the mild-mannered Vishnu holds the discus known as Sudarshana Chakra, considered the most destructive of all weapons.

VISHNU – THE PRESERVER GOD

Temple carving of Vishnu in his Ananda Sayana position

Vishnu is the highest and most immediate of all the energies of Brahman, the embodied Brahman, formed of the whole Brahman. On him this entire universe is woven and interwoven: from him is the world, and the world is in him; and he is the whole universe. Vishnu, the Lord, consisting of what is perishable as well as what is imperishable, sustains everything, both Spirit and Matter, in the form of his ornaments and weapons.

—VISHNU PURANA

❖ ❖ ❖

10

Alexander Conquers India and Retreats

Standing over 35 m in height, the Bamiyan Buddhas of Afghanistan are famous for their size, beauty, and craftsmanship. They were carved out from sandstone cliffs back in the sixth century CE and were the world's tallest Buddhas until 2001 CE. These monumental figures were annihilated with dynamite by the Taliban-led regime of that time in a blatant act of cultural vandalism that shocked the world. Today, plans are afoot to resurrect these famous figures to their original glory. The two Buddhas, draped in stucco robes, were testimony to classical blended style of Gandhara art that flourished in the region.

How did these statues of Buddha come to be carved in Muslim Afghanistan? In ancient times the region was known as Gandhara, and no Islamic presence existed there. In fact Islam arrived only after the seventh century CE. Earlier, we mentioned that Vedic people lived in the region that today comprises the nations of India, Pakistan, and Afghanistan. We also noted that around 500 BCE, people were challenging the authority of the Vedas, and Buddhism and Jainism were beginning to emerge.

THE ASCENT OF VISHNU AND THE FALL OF BRAHMA

One of the Bamiyan Buddhas before it was destroyed in 2001

While Hindus, Buddhists, and Jains were competing for religious supremacy in the region, a major event took place: the invasion of Alexander the Great late in the fourth century BCE. After defeating the Persian Empire, he entered northwestern India by crossing the Hindu Kush range. Although the king of Gandhara and some smaller kingdoms welcomed his incursion, Alexander was met with strong resistance from others. One such kingdom was Pushkalavati (near modern Peshawar), which was ruled by Queen Cleophis. The queen and 7000 of her soldiers were killed in the battle, but the Greek troops also suffered many casualties. Alexander himself was wounded, a rare event in his eleven-year campaign for world domination.

Alexander's first major military confrontation in India, however, had been with Porus, who was not only a legendary warrior with exceptional skills but generous even in war. After seeing Porus's army, Alexander is said to have remarked, "I see at last a danger that matches my courage." In the battle that followed, Alexander's better-equipped army overcame Porus's troops. When the defeated king was captured and brought before Alexander, the Greek asked Porus how he would like to be treated. The proud Porus responded, "As befits me, like a king." Alexander was impressed by his adversary and allowed Porus to retain his kingdom. But soon after the encounter Alexander decided to end his campaign for world conquest and return to his homeland.

The brief Greek contact, however, had a significant influence on Northwest India, notably its art forms. The Gandhara school of art shows Greek influences on the figures of Hindu gods and Buddha with depictions of wavy hair, sandals, and drapery. The Bamiyan Buddhas were in fact examples of Gandhara art. A by-product of the invasion was the opening of trade routes between India and the West. The name India also originated from the Greek connection.

By the way, Porus and Queen Cleophis do not sound like Indian names, do they? These names come from Greek accounts. Indian accounts record Porus as the ancient king of Pauravas. As for Cleophis, the Indian version of her name is Kripa. Likewise, the Greek Alexander was Sikandar in Indian accounts.

> *We can't equate democracy with Christianity because the largest democracy on earth is India, which is primarily Hindu. The third largest democracy is Indonesia, which is Islamic. Democracy and freedom are not dependent on Christian beliefs.*
>
> —JIMMY CARTER, 1924-

11

The Renaissance of Hinduism

> *The more superficially one studies Buddhism, the more it seems to differ from the Brahmanism in which it originated; the more profound our study, the more difficult it becomes to distinguish Buddhism from Brahmanism.*
>
> —ANANDA COOMARASWAMY, 1877-1947

According to the Pew Research Center, the Hindu population is expected to grow, if current demographic trends continue, from 1.03 billion to 1.38 billion by the midcentury. That's remarkable for a religion that was once about to be consigned to the garbage heap of posterity. By 500 BCE Hinduism was on life support. The authority of the Vedas was being questioned, and new religions like Buddhism and Jainism were becoming popular. Yet Hinduism made a remarkable turnaround, although it needed a long runway to relaunch itself. In fact the centuries that followed became the golden era of Hinduism, coinciding with the golden age of India. A tremendous amount of religious literature was composed during this period and led to a Hindu renaissance

THE ASCENT OF VISHNU AND THE FALL OF BRAHMA

that established it as the dominant religion of the region. In book 1 of this series, we discussed events before 500 BCE. This chapter discusses the development of Hinduism after 500 BCE, a span that encompasses several periods, some overlapping, as the table shows:

Epic Period	400 BCE – 400 CE
Epic and Classical Periods	400 BCE – 500 CE
Gupta Dynasty	300–500 CE (Golden Age of India)
Puranic Period	100–1000 CE

At about the time of Buddha (563–483 BCE), the concept of dharma, which is central to Hinduism, became expressed in a genre of texts known as the Dharmasutras and Dharmashastras. While the Sutras were a series of short sentences about dharma, the Shastras were more detailed treatises. The most significant was the Manusmriti, or the Laws of Manu, which was completed only in 200 CE. The Manusmriti explained the duties and responsibilities of the four different *varnas* (castes) at different stages of life. For instance, Brahmins were given the responsibility of teaching the Vedas and performing Vedic rituals. Furthermore, they were afforded great respect, for murder of a Brahmin was considered one of the greatest offenses against dharma. That the Dharmashastras heavily favored the Brahmins was no surprise because the Brahmins themselves wrote and compiled them. The caste system described in these works highlighted a rigid social stratification that later caused great difficulties. After the invasion of Alexander the Great, incursions from the northwest of India became more frequent, bringing with them many different people, including Bactrians, Scythians, Parthians, and Huns. But the Laws of Manu became an obstacle and none of them could be absorbed into Hinduism at the highest level of Brahmins. Some compromise was eventually made, and they were accepted into the Kshatriya caste (kings, military nobility, and warriors).

While the Brahmins were codifying the dharma literature, two major epics—the Ramayana and the Mahabharata—were being compiled and would change the religious landscape forever. The epics focused on the gods Shiva and Vishnu and moved away from the emphasis on Vedic gods. While the dharma literature focused on theory, the epics dealt with dharma in practice and highlighted the inner conflicts that arise when people try to follow all the dictates of dharma. With more than 100,000 two-line stanzas, the Mahabharata is the longest poem in the world. It is eight times longer than Homer's *Iliad* and *Odyssey* combined. The Ramayana is much shorter, with about 25,000 verses. The two epics mention the various kings and kingdoms of the time, but the historical accounts are still debated. The Mahabharata lists 3102 BCE as the year of the 18-day Kurukshetra War, the principal theme of the Mahabharata. Again, scholars do not agree on the accuracy of this date—most believe the war occurred around 1000 BCE. In general the epics highlight India's love of entertaining tales with characters entwined in complex human relationships. In the 1980s, when Indian national television broadcast episodes from the two main epics every Sunday morning, the whole nation would come to a complete stop—including motor and railroad traffic, for no one wanted to miss the program.

The Mahabharata contained two appendixes—the Bhagavad Gita and the Harivamsa—that became important sources of later mythological developments. The worship of Vishnu gained prominence during the epics through the incarnations of Krishna (Mahabharata) and Rama (Ramayana). The Vedic Rudra also gained importance and emerged as Shiva in the Shvetashvatara Upanishad, which describe him as creator, preserver, and destroyer of the universe. Although goddesses played minor roles in the Vedic era, they—particularly Lakshmi and Durga, as consorts of Vishnu and Shiva—became important in this period. Despite the significance attached to goddesses, major development of Shaktism did not take place until medieval times (500—1500 CE).

Yet another body of literature, the Puranas, which further elaborate Hindu mythology, was composed during this period. There were 18 main

Puranas, which include the Bhagavata Purana and the Vishnu Purana, and an equal number of subsidiary Puranas. While the major Puranas were compiled from 100 to 1000 CE, the subsidiary Puranas were written later. Although the Puranas describe the development of religion from the time of the Vedas to 100 CE, they also discuss genealogy and cosmology, among other things. It is from the Puranas we get the date of the Mahabharata war. These works show the tendency of Puranic authors to subject Vedic gods to ever-increasing moral weaknesses. The Puranas also describe in detail the ten avatars of Vishnu, known as Dashavataras.[19]

After Alexander died in 323 BCE, Chandragupta Maurya, the founder of the Mauryan dynasty, became the ruler of a vast empire that encompassed most of the Indian subcontinent. The early Mauryan rulers were liberal when it came to religion. In fact Chandragupta Maurya became a monk in later life and fasted to death in the Jain tradition. The most famous among the Mauryan rulers was undoubtedly Ashoka Maurya (ca. 268–232 BCE), who was greatly influenced by Buddhism. Ashoka did little to expand his kingdom during his reign; rather he spent his time sending Buddhist emissaries throughout Asia and commissioning some of the finest works of ancient Indian art. The Ashoka Chakra was created by the emperor and can be found today at the center of the National Flag of India.

Ashoka Chakra at the center of the Indian flag

---

[19] Books 3 and 4 in this series address the Dashavataras.

THE RENAISSANCE OF HINDUISM

Although many Hindu works were being compiled during this period, Buddhism was the dominant religion, its popularity boosted by the patronage of the emperor Ashoka. Most historians have only praise for Ashoka and describe him as one of the two greatest monarchs of ancient India (the other is Akbar of the Mughal dynasty). Even though both Ashoka and Akbar were warriors, their liberal attitude about religions other than their own was far ahead of their times and not seen anywhere in the world. Ashoka's patronage helped spread Buddhism, yet he was also respectful of Brahmins, as reflected in inscriptions on rock surfaces and pillars from this period. After Ashoka's death the empire shrank as a result of invasions, defections, and infighting. Toward the end of the Mauryan period, the first surviving stone images of Hinduism appeared. Hindu temples of that period were made of wood and did not last. Freestanding stone-and-brick temples soon arrived under the Gupta dynasty, which is often described as the golden age of India.

After the Mauryan dynasty collapsed in 185 BCE, the empire fragmented into many kingdoms. The first major consolidation did not occur for more than five hundred years, until Chandra Gupta (not to be confused with Chandragupta Maurya) rose to power in 320 CE. A significant milestone of the Gupta period was the development of temple architecture from stone and brick. The styles of temple architecture in North and South India also became more distinctive during this period.

The rise of the Gupta Empire saw the development of the great traditions of Vaishnavism (the most dominant Hindu sect), Shaivism, and Shaktism, and these would remain entrenched in the Hindu society. With the support of the Gupta emperors, Vaishnavas built numerous Vishnu temples. A spectacular carving at the rock-cut caves of Udayagiri in Madhya Pradesh dating to 400 CE depicts Varaha[20] rescuing the earth goddess.

Temples at Udayagiri and Deogarh also portray Vishnu's Ananda Sayana. The Gupta dynasty is credited with bringing Indian culture to

---

[20] We will describe Varaha in book 3 of this series.

Vishnu in his boar (Varaha) avatar, Udayagiri Caves

Southeast Asia. The later Gupta rulers worshipped Shiva, who was known by many names, such as Pashupati, Rudra, and Mahadeva. While the worshippers of Vishnu were concentrated in the North, Shiva worshippers were found in large numbers in the South.

The Gupta period is often regarded as the golden age of India. With Gupta's patronage, Hinduism became a leading religion of the subcontinent. Buddhism lost its popularity and struggled to remain afloat in India. People did not accept the austerity of Buddhism because the religion put the entire burden of salvation on the individual. The religion became popular only after the Mahayana faith espoused Hindu practices, such as the use of images for worship and priests for conducting rituals. Buddhism soon disappeared from most of the subcontinent, surviving only in the countries to which it had spread, including Sri Lanka and Southeast Asia.

THE RENAISSANCE OF HINDUISM

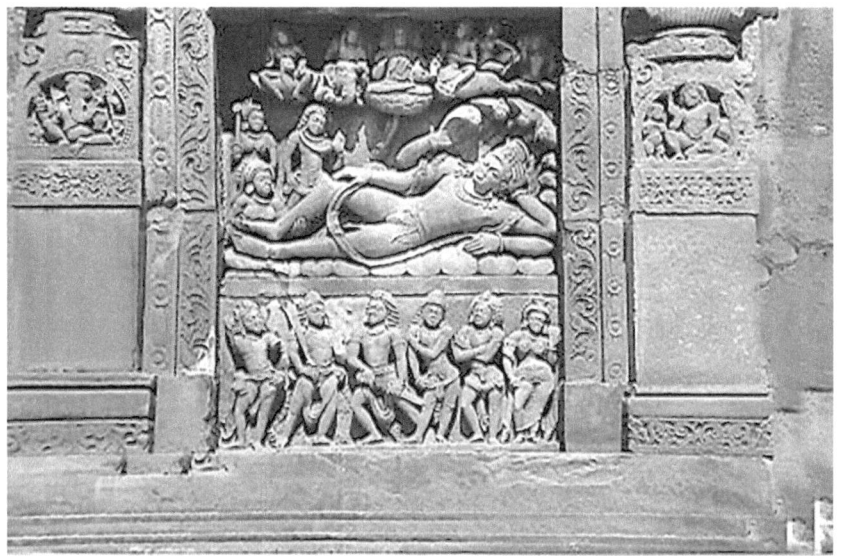

Ananda Sayana of Vishnu at the Dashavatara Temple, Deogarh, India

> *When I say that Buddhism is a part of Hinduism, certain people criticize me. But if I were to say that Hinduism and Buddhism are totally different, it would not be in conformity with truth.*
>
> —DALAI LAMA

12

Vishnu Sahasranama – The Thousand Names of Vishnu

In more than 100,000 stanzas the Mahabharata tells the story of a bitter battle between two clans of a royal family in northern India. One family is the virtuous Pandavas comprising five brothers led by Arjuna, the hero of the Bhagavad Gita. Fighting them are their evil cousins, the Kauravas, and the one hundred sons of a blind king. The war lasted only 18 days, but it left the capital city in utter ruin and nearly all the combatants dead.[21] Just as Arjuna was caught in a moral dilemma at the beginning of the war, Yudhishthira, his oldest brother, was devastated at its end by the death of his cousins, uncles, and teachers. While Arjuna looked up to Krishna for moral guidance, his older brother turned to their wise grandfather, Bhishma, who himself was on his deathbed, lying on a bed of arrows. The Vishnu Sahasranama offers the crux of this conversation between Bhishma and Yudhishthira. If the Bhagavad Gita is about our inner conflicts, the Vishnu Sahasranama is about the dharma of a Hindu.

---

[21] We will discuss the Mahabharata in detail in book 4 of this series.

THE ASCENT OF VISHNU AND THE FALL OF BRAHMA

Bhishma's last moments on a bed of arrows, artist unknown

But the Vishnu Sahasranama is nothing like the law books of Manu, which prescribe the duties and responsibilities of each caste. In essence the Vishnu Sahasranama is a list of one thousand names of Vishnu, with each name a tribute to his manifold qualities.[22] That makes the Vishnu Sahasranama both practical and philosophical. Originally it was part of the Anushasana Parva, or Book of Instructions, of the Mahabharata. It was subsequently listed in other sacred texts, such as the Padma Purana, Skanda Purana, and Garuda Purana. The Vishnu Sahasranama is considered one of the most sacred *stotras* (hymns of praise) in Hinduism.

The origin of the Vishnu Sahasranama is a question posed by Yudhishthira in the aftermath of the Mahabharata War. Yudhishthira is the son of Dharma (Yama, the god of the dead) and has a natural ability to discern right from wrong. Yet he is greatly distressed at the death of his kinsmen and is completely unable to understand the meaning of

---

[22] Sometimes the number of names is given as 1,008.

life. He asks Bhishma, from whom he learned sacred lore, about the greatest dharma that allows a Hindu to escape the cycle of deaths and rebirths.

Bhishma responds by chanting the Vishnu Sahasranama. For Bhishma the main path to moksha is devotion. The one thousand names describe only a handful of Vishnu's infinite attributes, for the names Pitambara ("vested in yellow"), Damodara ("rope around the belly"), or Gopala ("protector of cows") are only some of the roles played by Vishnu in his incarnations. At first Bhishma's answer may appear to be simplistic, but couched in his response was one of the profound wisdoms that formed the framework of devotion for the Vaishnavas. The Vaishnavas believe Brahman as Vishnu pervades the entire cosmos as a cosmic spirit, and a part of this cosmic spirit resides in each human soul. Furthermore, they believe this spirit associates with the soul through devotion. Thus devotion is a central tenet of Vaishnavas, who are committed to such practices as singing *bhajans* (devotional songs) and chanting hymns.

The Vishnu Sahasranama has attracted plenty of commentary from renowned philosophers of ancient India. In the eighth century Adi Shankara, well known for his contributions to the doctrine of Advaita Vedanta, wrote a commentary about the Sahasranama that became influential in many other schools of Hinduism. The 12th century Vaishnava teacher Parasara Bhattar, a follower of Ramanuja, a Hindu theologian, believed that Vishnu Sahasranama absolves devotees of all sins and has no equal. According to the 14th century Dvaita philosopher Madhava, each name in the Sahasranama is so profound that it has more than a hundred meanings.[23] For Swami Tapasyananda of the Ramakrishna Mission organization, "nothing evil or inauspicious will befall a man here or hereafter who daily hears or repeats these names."

---

[23] Advaita and Dvaita, meaning nondualistic and dualistic respectively, are opposing schools of thought in Hinduism. Advaitas believe the universal soul (Brahman) and the individual soul (atman) are one and the same. Dvaitas, on the other hand, believe they are different.

THE ASCENT OF VISHNU AND THE FALL OF BRAHMA

The Vishnu Sahasranama has also invited some controversy because the one thousand names of Vishnu include Shiva and Rudra—which has intrigued many Shaivites and others. Most Vaishnavas, however, interpret the name Shiva as referring to "one who bestows auspiciousness" and not the deity itself. Other traditions, however, believe that Vishnu and Shiva are one and same, and popular names like Shankaranarayana and Harihara attest to this unity.

A thousand names also exist for other deities like Shiva, Lalita (Devi), and Ganesha. Yet the most popular among them is unquestionably the Vishnu Sahasranama, for Vishnu and his avatars command more devotees than any other Hindu denomination. A little-known fact is that the Vishnu Sahasranama is recited more often than the Bhagavad Gita, even though both originated in the same source, the Mahabharata.

> *Through our chanting we merge our personal consciousness momentarily with the infinite consciousness that is our origin and our destiny. It is the drop of water finding its way back into the ocean from which it came.*
>
> —VICTOR SHAMAS

13

How Dhruva Became the Unwavering Polaris

He who rules by moral force is like the pole star, which remains in place while all the lesser stars do homage to it.

–CONFUCIUS

The story of Dhruva is a tale of unwavering devotion of a child to his deity. Dhruva was the son of a Hindu king[24] who had two queens. One day Dhruva ran to sit in his father's lap, but the king shoved him away. The king instead picked up Dhruva's half-brother, the child of his favorite queen, and put him in his lap. Dhruva was inconsolable and ran to his mother's lap. She held him dearly and explained that because his half-brother had performed good deeds in his previous lives, he had earned the right to sit on the throne with his father. If Dhruva performed

---

[24] The king was Uttanapada, the son of Swayambhuva Manu (the first Manu, who became one of the architects of the caste system).

good deeds instead of moaning about his plight, he could also enjoy good fortune in the future.

Dhruva took his mother's advice to heart. He ran away to the forest to do penance so that he could earn enough karmic merit to sit on the highest throne with his father. On his way he met the wandering sage Narada, who explained to Dhruva that Vishnu is the real father of everyone. He initiated Dhruva in Vishnu's sacred mantra, "*Om Namo Bhagavate Vasudevaya!*" meaning "With loving reference, I surrender to Lord Vishnu."

Dhruva chose a secluded spot on the banks of a river and began his worship of Vishnu, chanting the mantra continuously. Such was the intensity of his penance that it caused a stir in the divine realm. Through his web of Indranet, Indra noticed a five-year-old performing severe penance that even adults have trouble sustaining. Indra became anxious, for he thought the boy was after his throne. The child was gaining power through his austerities, and Indra believed something had to be done immediately to disrupt the boy's penance. Soon Indra, disguised as Dhruva's mother, approached him and pleaded with him to give up his penance. But Dhruva was undeterred. Indra next let loose a pack of wild beasts on the boy, but that only made Dhruva double his resolve.

When the gods found themselves incapable of disrupting Dhruva's penance, they went to Vishnu and told him about the boy's intense devotion. Vishnu appeared before the child and watched him with utter fascination. Dhruva repeated the mantra with such innocent sincerity that Vishnu's heart melted. Vishnu picked the boy up and put him in his lap on the highest throne in the world.

There is no sky as big as the one that covers the ocean. Today Dhruva sits in this sky as the brightest and the most constant star. Because of his unwavering devotion to Vishnu, he was immortalized as the polestar. Also called the North Star and Polaris, the polestar is aligned with earth's axis of rotation. While other stars change their positions during the night, the polestar remains fixed.

HOW DHRUVA BECAME THE UNWAVERING POLARIS

Vishnu appearing before Dhruva, 19th century painting by Raja Ravi Varma

You can see Dhruva on a clear night, as a beacon guiding people at sea to their destination. Fools watch the waves and make decisions according to ever-changing circumstances, but a wise captain charts his course by a star that does not move. Dhruva is that beautiful, unwavering, constant Polaris in the boundless sky. In Hinduism Dhruva joins great devotees like Arjuna, Hanuman, and Prahlada. The word *dhruva* means "fixed" or "immovable in resolve," for Dhruva has become the embodiment of willpower.

In the Mahabharata, Dhruva is seen switching roles. As one of the eight Vasus (attendants of Indra and later Vishnu), he is cursed along

THE ASCENT OF VISHNU AND THE FALL OF BRAHMA

with other Vasus for stealing Vasishtha's cow. We will relate that story in book 4 of this series.

> *Be as the sailor who keeps the polestar in his eye.*
> *By so doing we may not arrive at our port within a*
> *calculable period, but we will maintain a true course.*
>
> —HENRY DAVID THOREAU, 1817-1862

14

Bhakti Sweeps India

I belong to no religion. My religion is love.
Every heart is a temple.

–RUMI, 1207-1273

The "spiritual" life is abuzz in India, which is home to some of the intoxicating liquors of the world, including the finest single-malt and blended whiskies. Although the fondness for the brew has been celebrated in Indian mythology by gods like Indra and Agni, India's alcohol consumption is fairly low because of religious and cultural reasons. In fact only a third of the country's billion-plus population drinks regularly. During Vedic times the most potent drink was undoubtedly soma, which was popularized by Indra and considered the source of his bravery. Another heady liquor that has been around for centuries is bhang, a concoction banned in many countries. A natural intoxicant made from the leaves and flowers of marijuana, bhang was used in religious rituals from ancient times and is particularly popular during the color festival of Holi. But the favorite of the sages of India and the mother of all intoxicating liquors is indisputably bhakti: the divine nectar that drowns your sorrow and makes even the most bitter experiences seem sweet. Throughout the millennia severe storms of religious ecstasy have struck India. The winds of bhakti and waves of ecstatic chanting have swept through the subcontinent like shock waves, and their aftermaths have revealed the simple truth that Hinduism is a religion of unwavering devotees deeply committed to their deities.

So what is bhakti? It is heartfelt devotion to a personal god.[25] Devotees are called *bhaktas*, and the spiritual journey through the heart is called Bhakti Yoga or Bhakti Marg. In the Bhagavad Gita Krishna says: "Be it a leaf, or flower, or fruit, or water that a zealous soul offer with love (bhakti), I willingly accept, for it was the love that made the offering." It appears god makes his gracious love available to anyone who approaches him, including outcastes and women, the groups excluded by the sage Manu. The divine relationship with the god can take many forms: father, mother, friend, or even an adversary. For Poonthanam, Krishna was his child, whereas the 15th century saint Mira Bai regarded Krishna as her lover (bridal mysticism). In an earlier chapter we described how much the demon Shishupala loathed Vishnu. Because Shishupala constantly thought about Vishnu, Shishupala achieved liberation after death.

The object of devotion need not always be a personal god; it can be a saint or even a guru. The Shvetashvatara Upanishad says:

> *He who has the highest bhakti of deva*
> *Like his Deva, so is his guru*
> *Who is high-minded to him*
> *These teachings will be illuminating.*

The devotion to a guru is evident in the story of Melpathur Bhattathiri, who was a staunch atheist earlier in his life but became a believer. As a testament to his relationship with his guru, he even welcomed his

---

[25] As we discussed earlier, a personal god is the same as Saguna Brahman.

guru's ailment (rheumatism) on himself as *guru-dakshina* (guru fees). We describe this story later in this book.

Although Shaivites, Shaktas, Smartas, and other Hindu denominations practice the notion of bhakti, it has a special significance for Vaishnavas, who consider it their guiding principle. For Vaishnavas an ounce of bhakti is worth a pound of knowledge. Vaishnavas also believe that bhakti is the fastest path to spiritual attainment. Bhakti Yoga is often likened to the jackfruit tree, which produces fruit at the bottom of the trunk that people can reach effortlessly. Compare this with a coconut tree, whose fruit people can reach only by climbing.

The bhakti movement originated in South India. Buddhism was becoming popular at that time, and Hindu priests realized they were losing devotees to Buddhism because Buddhist monks would speak the local language when engaging with members of the public, instead of speaking Pali, the language of Buddhist scriptures. Consequently the Hindu saints began to disseminate the wisdom of Upanishads and other religious texts to the masses in simple language, often resorting to poetry and witty aphorisms. Some saints also composed lyrics in local languages and set them to music. They encouraged the masses to sing and dance in devotion to Vishnu or Shiva.

Such devotional singing began in the Indian state of Tamil Nadu in the fourth through the ninth centuries, when a number of devotional mystics walked from village to village singing songs in a language people understood. The bhakti movement initially was spearheaded by the 12 Alvars (Vaishnava devotees) and 63 Nayanars (Shaiva devotees), who together were often revered as the 75 apostles of bhakti. Prominent among the Alvars was Andal, the lone female saint, who offered the best expressions of bridal mysticism in Hinduism. Among the Nayanars, the famous saints were Sambandar, Appar, and Sundarar, who, along with the ninth-century saint-poet Manikkavachakar, composed devotional hymns that were both ecstatic and touching.

The bhakti movement spread from Tamil Nadu to Karnataka and Maharashtra during the 12th and 13th centuries. Basava, a prominent

12th century Karnataka saint, was a devotee of Shiva and one of the great religious reformers in Hindu history. He led the Shaivites in rejecting caste distinctions and honoring women as equal to men. Another famous saint was the Vishnu devotee Purandara Dasa of the 15th century, who was well known for his contributions to Carnatic music. In the state of Maharashtra, the most celebrated of the bhakti saints was the 13th century Jnanadeva,[26] who was famous for his commentary on the Bhagavad Gita. The bhakti movement also spread to the central regions of India, and was then carried by Hindu pilgrims to Varanasi in the North, where Hindi-speaking saints popularized the cult of devotion across the countryside.

Between the 14th and 17th centuries, when North India was under Muslim domination, a massive bhakti wave swept through this region and was initiated by a loose association of teachers or saints, including Chaitanya, Vallabha, Mira Bai, Tulsi Das, and Tukaram. They exhorted people to set aside caste and rituals and to express their overwhelming love of their god. Unlike its southern counterparts, the bhakti movement in the North did not have anything like the Alvars and Nayanars. While the South Indian devotional movement was focused on Shiva, Vishnu, and his incarnations, the North Indian movement was centered on Rama and Krishna. Because the bhakti movement eschewed caste distinctions and disregarded Brahmanic rituals, it initially was considered unorthodox and not crucial for salvation. However, because of its immense popularity it eventually became one of the important modes of religious expression in modern India.

The bhakti movement led to the birth of an entire genre of saints. It witnessed a surge in Hindu literature in regional languages and led to the development of vernacular languages all over the country. The movement became richer with the practice of converting entire texts of Ramayana, Mahabharata, and Bhagavata Purana to musical recitation. The movement also gave rise to a renaissance in music, as devotional

---

[26] Jnanadeva is also known as Jnaneshwar or Dnyaneshwar.

songs were sung not only in traditional places like temples but also in special music halls.

Yet the bhakti movement is not without controversies. Scholars often debate whether bhakti is a reform movement or the natural progression of Hindu thought. Bhakti is not Vedic, and it appears, somewhat suddenly and unheralded, in the Shvetashvatara Upanishad and the Bhagavad Gita. Most scholars, however, contend that the movement is not reformist or representative of a rebellion or rapid innovation but a revival of ancient Vedic traditions. Its period of greatest prominence coincided with the Muslim penetration of northern India. Whether this flowering of devotional poetry would have occurred without the existence of Islam is another contentious issue. Quite likely it was a reaction that occurred among Hindus when their saints realized the Muslim Sufi dervishes and saints were becoming increasingly popular because they spoke to the masses in their languages and sang and danced in devotion to Allah.

In the final analysis, the bhakti movement was a devotional transformation of medieval Hindu society. It upended the traditional dynamics of worship. The greatest gift of the bhakti movement was making god accessible to low caste and outcast people for whom conversion to Islam had been the only way of achieving spiritual contentment.

> *Love is the song of the soul singing to God.*
> —PARAMAHAMSA YOGANANDA, 1893-1952

15

The Abode of Gods – Temples

The doorstep to the temple of wisdom is a knowledge of our own ignorance.

–BENJAMIN FRANKLIN, 1706-1790

India is universally known as the land of spiritual awakening and is home to some of the most ancient temples of the world. To an outsider, however, Indian temples may look strange, with many multi-limbed deities decorated in lavish costumes and served with food. To the architect and aesthetic they might even look grotesque, with nothing in common with the great cathedrals of Europe. But that's hardly surprising because Indian civilization is a giant river that has been flowing nonstop for 5000 years, and during its course it has absorbed many cultural tributaries, both turbid and clear. Even with the brief Hellenic contact about 2300 years ago, the long-standing Islamic influence that began in the 13th century, and the British colonization of India from the 18th century, the main current had always traveled along native tracks. The Indian temple is a product of this insularity in the face of constant incursions. Like the

Pyramids of Egypt or the Parthenon of Athens, it has remained remarkably indigenous.

Despite the presence of many illustrious deities, no temples existed in the Vedic period. The main object of worship was fire in honor of Agni. Central to all Vedic rites, the holy fire was lit on a platform in the open air, and oblations were offered. As the Vedic age progressed, the concept of a temple began to take shape. The temple was the residence of god, and the deity was placed on a pedestal, ready to receive the prayers and gifts from the devout. In this context a deity was not unlike a monarch seated on a throne, receiving tributes and petitions from subjects. Larger temples were usually built at picturesque places, especially on riverbanks, hilltops, or seashores. Smaller temples or open-air shrines were located just about anywhere—by the roadside or even under a tree. Most holy places in India are famous for its temples. Towns from Amarnath in the North or to Kanyakumari at India's southern tip are renowned for their magnificent temples.

Although 82 percent of the Indian population is Hindu, an Indian temple is not necessarily a Hindu shrine. India also has Buddhist, Jain, and Sikh temples. All temples are built to enshrine images of gods or saints, except the Sikh temple, or *gurdwara*, where the only object of veneration is the sacred book called Guru Granth Sahib, a collection of teachings and writings by Guru Nanak and others. In the case of a Buddhist temple, the object of worship is often a relic mound called a *stupa* or an image of Buddha. In Jain temples the presiding deity can be any or all of the 24 *tirthankaras*, who are deified saints. In Hindu temples an important god or goddess of the pantheon becomes the object of worship. Most Hindu temples are dedicated to members of the Hindu Trinity, and many temples of Vishnu and Shiva exist throughout India. As we have explained, only a few temples are dedicated to Brahma.

The main object of worship in a Shiva temple is usually the *linga*, a cylindrical stone symbolizing cosmic energy. Shiva is also worshipped as Nataraja, the king of dance, particularly in South India. In fact the cosmic dance of Shiva has inspired some of the finest masterpieces of

Indian sculpture. The chief deity in Vishnu temples is an image of the god in any of the 24 iconographic forms (based on placement of objects like weapons) or the ten earthly incarnations, which include Krishna and Rama. Ganesha, the son of Shiva, is a popular deity worshipped throughout India and abroad. Still other temples are dedicated to the consorts of Vishnu and Shiva.

According to Hindu beliefs, Shiva resides at the summit of Mount Kailash, where he sits in constant meditation along with his wife, Parvati. Vishnu, on the other hand, resides in his celestial city called Vaikuntha, which is in the direction of the Capricorn constellation. Accompanied by his wife, Lakshmi, and the giant snake Shesha, Vishnu is in perpetual slumber. Both Kailash and Vaikuntha are mythical places. The physical representations of gods that adorn the niches, walls, and towers of temples have earthly trappings. The craftsmen who fashioned the temples and their sculptures depicted the gods as symbols of power. The sculptors were confined in their work by rigid rules about iconography, such as what goes in the right hand, yet the gods tend to look young and handsome and are often seen in smiling or serene postures. And they are usually draped in rich apparel or adorned with expensive jewelry.

Hindu temples are sacred places for devotees to pay homage to their favorite deities. No sermons are delivered there. There are no lectures on morality or religious education. However, not every Hindu visits a temple regularly because in Hinduism, a temple visit is not mandatory. Most Hindus, however, have their own smaller versions of temples at home. The home shrine, often the *puja* room, is used for daily prayers. Hindus usually visit temples on auspicious occasions or during religious festivals. Hindu temples also do not play a crucial role in marriages and funerals.

Before we leave this topic, we list the famous temples of India according to their popularity and history. Hindu mythology often mentions these places of worship, so they will appear from time to time in this narrative.

Famous Temples of India

1	**Kashi Vishwanath** Location: Varanasi, Uttar Pradesh	One of the holiest temples of India and dedicated to Shiva. The temple was destroyed and re-constructed a number of times in history. The last structure was demolished by Aurangzeb for a mosque and later reconstructed on a nearby site by the Maratha monarch, Ahilya Bai Holkar. The temple stands on the western bank of the holy river Ganga and holds utmost importance for the Hindus, who believe that a bath in river can liberate them from all sins.
2	**Jagannath Temple** Location: Puri, Odisha	Massive temple consisting of 120 shrines. The temple is one of the oldest and an important pilgrimage destination for many Hindu traditions, particularly worshippers of Krishna and Vishnu, and part of the Char Dham pilgrimage. Unlike other deities that are made of stone or metal, the image of Jagannath is made out of wood and are replaced every 12 or 19 years. The temple was built in the 12th century and is famous for its annual Ratha Yatra, or chariot festival, in which the three main temple deities are hauled on elaborately decorated chariots
3	**Tirumala Venkateswara Temple** Location: Tirupati, Andhra Pradesh	The important shrine of Venkateswara, a form of Vishnu, is the richest temple in the world in terms of donations received. With around 40 million annual visitors, it is also the most visited religious place in the world. The temple uses Dravidian architecture.

4	**Vaishno Devi Temple** Location: Jammu	A notable Hindu temple situated on top of the Trikuta Mountains. The temple is dedicated to Vaishno Devi, a manifestation of goddess Lakshmi. It is the second most visited temple in the country with more 10 million visitors per year.
5	**Somnath Temple** Location: Saurashtra, Gujarat	Dedicated to Shiva, the temple is first among the twelve Jyotirlinga shrines of Shiva. Legend has it that the temple was built by the moon god Chandra after Shiva freed him from the curse of waning. The temple has destroyed several times by Islamic kings and rebuilt as many times by Hindu kings.
6	**Siddhivinayak Temple** Location: Mumbai, Maharashtra	Built in the year 1801, the Siddhivinayak temple is a prominent temple dedicated to Ganesha. The inner roof of the temple complex is plated with gold. This is one of the richest temples of Mumbai and frequented by Bollywood stars for good luck.
7	**Ramanathaswamy Temple** Location: Rameswaram, Tamil Nadu	One of the most popular temples of the south, Ramanathaswamy temple is the abode of Shiva. It is also one of the twelve Jyotirlingas of Shiva in the country. Legend has it that Rama, the seventh incarnation of god Vishnu, prayed to Shiva to absolve of the sin of killing a Brahmin—Ravana, the demon king of Lanka.
8	**Shirdi Sai Baba Temple** Location: Ahmednagar, Maharashtra	The holy shrine of Sai Baba, the Indian spiritual master revered by both Hindus and Muslims and widely regarded as a saint, fakir, and satguru. The temple is the third richest in India.

9	**Padmanabhaswamy Temple** Location: Thiruvananthapuram, Kerala	The temple is dedicated to Vishnu and the principal deity is enshrined in the Ananda Sayana posture. Based on Dravidian style architecture, the temple is mentioned in many Puranas and is said to at least 5000 years old. It is the richest temple of India in terms of assets ($21 billion USD).
10	**Meenakshi Amman Temple** Location: Madurai, Tamil Nadu	The temple is dedicated to Meenakshi, an avatar of Parvati, and her consort, Shiva (Sundareswar). Unlike most Shiva temples of South India, Meenakshi is the principal deity, and not Shiva. Meenakshi was born with three breasts, and legend has it that her extra breast would disappear after she meets her future husband.

> *This is my simple religion. There is no need for temples; no need for complicated philosophy. Our own brain, our own heart is our temple; the philosophy is kindness.*
>
> —DALAI LAMA

16

Vaishnavism – The Most Dominant Sect of Hinduism

If Hinduism is an umbrella of traditions, then the longest shadow is cast by the Vaishnava tradition. It is the largest Hindu denomination with almost seven hundred million adherents. Sometimes known as Vaishnavites, Vaishnavas regard Vishnu or one of his incarnations as the supreme deity. They respect most sacred texts of mainstream Hinduism, but they especially revere the Bhagavad Gita, the Bhagavata Purana, the Vishnu Purana, and the Gita Govinda because these texts focus on Vishnu or his incarnations Krishna and Rama. Vaishnavism is rich not only in religious literature but also in temples and saints.

A distinctive feature of Vaishnavism is its emphasis on bhakti and morality. Although Vaishnavism recognizes the importance of meditation or philosophical contemplation, its focus is on the heart, not the mind. Vaishnava look upon the supreme deity as a personal being with whom they can have an intimate relationship. The ancient Vedic term Purushottama means "ultimate person" and is often used to describe the human attributes of a god. Vaishnavas also use the term *bhava* (emotion) to describe the overwhelming joy they experience in the close company of a personal god, particularly through devotional singing and ecstatic chanting. Many Vaishnavas also consider Lakshmi, the consort of Vishnu, equal to or more powerful than Vishnu. She is another aspect of the ultimate reality and often is called Sri, the auspicious one.

Vaishnavism has several subsects, each based on the relationship between the universal soul (Brahman) and the individual soul (atman). Vaishnavas in general believe that the universal soul is separate from the individual soul, but the varying degrees of separation between these souls have led to the creation of many philosophical sects within the tradition. The philosopher Madhava and his followers, for instance, believe that atman is dependent on Brahman. The Gaudiya sect, founded by the 15th century Bengali saint Chaitanya, believes that Brahman and atman are different and that their relationship is beyond the scope of human comprehension. A famous devotee from the Gaudiya sect was Swami Prabhupada, best known as the founder of the Hare Krishna movement.

The members of the various sects within the Vaishnavas can be identified by the style of the mark worn on the forehead of devotees. Called *tilak*, the mark is usually made of sandalwood paste and generally applied vertically for Vaishnavas and horizontally for Shaivites.[27] Even among Vaishnavites the vertical lines are drawn in various styles and can represent a *U*, *Y*, or *T* to denote a particular sect of Vaishnavism.

How did Vaishnavism become popular? It started to flourish in predominantly Shaivite South India between the fourth and ninth centuries as a result of the 12 Alvar saints, who traveled on foot from village to village, singing songs and chanting hymns composed in local languages. The Alvars showed that intense devotion can transport the human soul to the highest states of mystical ecstasy. Saturated with love for the divine, the bhakti movement became popular among common people and soon spread to the North of the country, where Hindi-speaking saints

---

[27] The Shaivite *tilak* typically appears as three horizontal lines called Tripundra and drawn on the forehead with ashes.

popularized the cult of devotion. The Alvars had such a profound impact on Hindu spirituality that intellectuals across the country were forced to rethink their philosophical systems to accommodate a personable god. Vaishnavism became even more significant in later years through the influence of saints like Mira Bai, Chaitanya, Tulsi Das, Tukaram, and others.

Vaishnavas are famous for their loud expressions of devotion. The sect is well known for singing devotional songs called *bhajans* in groups. A famous *bhajan* is "Vaishnava Jana To," composed by the 15th century poet Narsi Mehta from Gujarat and acclaimed as highly inspirational. The song was popularized by Mahatma Gandhi, who sang it every day and believed it carried the essence of Hindu philosophy.

We mentioned earlier that Vaishnavism has produced a number of saints over the years. In the chapters that follow we will focus on some of the ancient saints. The saints Andal and Mira Bai were exponents of bridal mysticism. We also describe the interesting story of the little-known South Indian saint Poonthanam. The dancing saint Chaitanya is discussed in book 4 of this series, in the context of Krishna. Vaishnavas' places of worship are scattered throughout the subcontinent and include the world-famous Angkor Wat in Cambodia and the Jagannath Temple in Odisha, India. We will discuss some of them in the next few chapters.

A Vaishnava is personally tolerant for the benefit of others. His lack of prowess should not be construed as lacking in strength; rather, it shows his tolerance for the welfare of the entire human society.

–A. C. BHAKTIVEDANTA SWAMI PRABHUPADA, 1896-1977

17

Vishnu Is Not Easy to Impress

Of the gods in the Trimurti, guess who is the easiest to please? Vishnu? Not a chance. Shiva? Not quite. The answer is Brahma, followed by Shiva, and lastly Vishnu. Hindu mythology is full of stories of Brahma happily dishing out boons, then scurrying to Shiva or Vishnu to reverse them. That does not mean Shiva is not susceptible to flattery. Although a legitimate amount of penance can flatter Shiva, Vishnu is especially hard to please and seldom grants wishes even to his staunchest devotees. But when Vishnu is pleased—however long that might take—he'll bestow the greatest riches on a devotee, as the stories of Kuchela, Dhruva, and Prahlada attest.

One such fervent devotee of Vishnu was Narada. For those who don't know him, Narada is a sage of multiple talents, better known as a traveling musician-cum-storyteller who goes about the universe touting his lord's glories and playing devotional music. Sporting a knotted tuft of hair at the center of his scalp, he makes his characteristic appearance uttering the words, *"Narayana, Narayana"* (one of Vishnu's names), and carrying a veena. When not involved in musical pursuits, he turns into a mischievous gossip monger, divulging the personal plans of deities and thereby stirring controversies. Although he has no malicious intent, his deeds unwittingly invite trouble and friction among gods, demons, and people.

Once Narada took a break from his busy travel schedule and headed to the mountains, where he undertook extreme penance for many years. His intense meditation caught the attention of Indra, who was worried that the power Narada gained through penance could be used to overthrow him. Indra dispatched Kama, the lord of love, to disrupt Narada's meditation. Kama had once broken the supreme concentration of Shiva. Kama turned a snow-capped mountain into a grove of pine trees and the ungainly shrubs into flowering vines. In these serene settings he made the attractive *apsaras* dance. He then released floral arrows aimed at the sage from his sugarcane bow. But Narada was unperturbed and did not even open his eyes. Having failed in his attempt, Kama prostrated at Narada's feet and begged for mercy. Only the spiritually powerful are able to resist Kama.

When Narada opened his eyes, he realized what had happened. He felt an overwhelming sense of pride about his ability to withstand Kama. Narada headed to Kailash, where Shiva came out to meet Narada and congratulate him on his achievement. When Narada was about to leave, Shiva warned him not to mention what had happened to Vishnu. But Narada was a sworn devotee of Vishnu's. In his next meeting with Vishnu, Narada disregarded Shiva's words of caution and with great pride related his victory over Kama.

Soon thereafter Narada returned to his traveling ways, strumming his veena as he went. He came upon a beautiful city where the local king, Shilanidhi, received him with great honor. When the king's daughter, Srimati, approached Narada to wash his feet, the sage couldn't help noticing how strikingly beautiful she was. She had large, shining eyes and looked exactly like his lord's wife, Lakshmi. The flames of desire set the sage on fire, even though he had taken a vow to remain celibate. When the king announced that a *swayamvara* had been arranged for his daughter, Narada became pensive. He thought it was time he ended his solitary life and settled down.

For the next few days Narada couldn't stop thinking about the girl. The love-struck sage thought about courting Srimati at the *swayamvara*. He was proud of his ascetic powers and had proved himself more powerful than both Kama and Shiva. Then he became worried. What if Srimati did not reciprocate his feelings and did not find him attractive? Narada prayed to Vishnu to turn him into a handsome prince so that Srimati would choose him at the *swayamvara*. When Vishnu appeared before his devotee, Narada pleaded, "Please grant me a face like Hari's." "So be it," Vishnu said and disappeared, for Hari was another name of Vishnu.

Kings and princes from far and wide attended the *swayamvara*. Dressed as his usual ascetic self, Narada walked into the hall carrying his veena. He looked condescendingly upon the gathered suitors. When all had lined up for the *swayamvara*, Srimati entered the hall carrying a floral garland. She looked at each suitor and walked past each one until she came face to face with Narada, who was standing near the end. She looked even prettier than usual in her wedding garments. Narada tried hard not to stare, but in her crystal-clear round eyes he could see his own reflection—his tuft of hair and his veena, but with a monkey face. "What! That couldn't be me!" As she looked at Narada, Srimati suddenly burst into laughter. Before Narada realized what had happened, Srimati had moved on and garlanded the prince next to him, who looked like Vishnu reincarnated.

Utterly embarrassed, Narada was consumed by anger and betrayal. He had been reduced to a laughingstock in front of many kings and princes. Why would his own beloved deity, whom he had worshipped throughout his life, give him a monkey head and let him down so badly? Because he was unable to marry the love of his life, Narada cursed Vishnu to suffer the agony of being separated from his spouse and the ignobility of having monkeys as his allies.

As a lifelong devotee of Vishnu, Narada believed he was entitled to his wish. But Vishnu had realized that Narada was consumed by pride and considered himself superior to Shiva. Although Narada was a beloved devotee of the god, he had deviated from the path of dharma. Granting his wish would only make him stray further. Vishnu had created the city of King Shilanidhi to bring Narada to his senses. The king's daughter, Srimati, was none other than Vishnu's wife, Lakshmi. When Narada asked for Hari's face, Vishnu played with the semantics—*Hari* can also mean "monkey," among other things—and gave Narada a monkey face. And the prince Srimati garlanded at the *swayamvara* was none other than Vishnu himself, disguised as a prince. Narada had no idea about the elaborate trap set up to curb his arrogance, for the ways of Vishnu are mysterious.

Severe penances or constant hosannas can earn a devotee instant rewards from Brahma or Shiva, but Vishnu is not easily pleased and his benediction often comes late.

> *Wealth and piety will decrease day by day, until the world will be wholly depraved. Then property alone will confer rank; wealth will be the only source of devotion; passion will be the sole bond of union between the sexes; falsehood will be the only means of success in litigation; and women will be objects merely of sensual gratification.*
>
> —VISHNU PURANA

❂ ❂ ❂

18

Anatomy of a Hindu Temple

Here's a question: Which among the following temples is the tallest?

1. Angkor Wat in Cambodia
2. Ranganathaswamy Temple in Trichy, Tamil Nadu
3. Swaminarayan Akshardham Temple in Delhi
4. Khajuraho Kandariya Mahadeva
5. Sun Temple of Konark

If you experienced a momentary brain fade, that's understandable. Unless you are the ultimate architect-cum-devotee with all the structural information at your fingertips, not many people know about the important Hindu temples let alone their heights. Although the focus of the book is Hindu mythology, at various stages we will be discussing some of the important Hindu temples, particularly from a mythological perspective. Most temples on the list belong to this category. They were also nominated as UNESCO World Heritage Sites. But before we address the question of heights, let's dissect a Hindu temple in more detail.

Although the temples of India are architecturally remote from the cathedrals of Europe, they have many interesting points of comparison. We mentioned earlier that Hindu temples evolved over two thousand years and differ in size and shape. They can be rectangular or octagonal or semicircular, and they have different types of domes and gates. The temples in southern India have a different style than those in northern India. In general the architecture of Indian temples can be classified as Nagara (northern), Dravida (southern), or Vesara (a hybrid). The Vesara architecture, which has a distinct air of importance but is not showy, can be found in the Deccan region of central India. But these are not the only styles. While most temples are in the Nagara or Dravida styles, those in Bengal, Kerala, and the Himalayan valley have their own distinct styles. Despite the differences, these temples have many features in common that become obvious when we draw our attention to the six parts of a Hindu temple.

The dome and steeple: The steeple of the dome—the equivalent of the spire of a gothic cathedral—is called a *shikhara*, or tower. It represents the mythological Mount Meru, that is, the highest mountain peak. Although the shape of the dome varies from region to region, the steeple is often in the form of the trident of Shiva. In South India the corresponding term for *shikhara* is *vimana*. But *vimanas* are different, and much smaller, than the elaborate South Indian temple gateway towers called *gopura*, which are perhaps the most prominent features of those temples. The tallest point of a North Indian temple is usually the *shikhara*, and for a South Indian temple it is the *gopura*.

The inner chamber: The inner chamber, or sanctum sanctorum, of the temple is called *garbha-griha*, or womb chamber, and corresponds to the chancel of a gothic cathedral. The main deity, usually carved in stone, resides in this chamber. The *shikhara* rises from the roof of the inner chamber. In most temples only temple priests are allowed to enter the *garbha-griha*. Visitors cannot enter this area. The doorway of the *garbha-griha* almost always faces east. Although the chief deity is directly under the *shikhara* of a North Indian temple or the *vimana* of a South Indian temple, it is never under the *gopura*.

The temple hall: Most large temples have a hall where devotees gather for worship. Devotees use the hall, called the *mandapa*, to meditate, pray, chant, or watch the priests perform rituals. The hall is usually made of pillars and decorated with sculptures or paintings of gods and goddesses. Sometimes the hall is also called the *nata-mandir* (dance hall), where women dancers, or *devadasis,* used to perform dance rituals.[28] Even the largest of the *mandapas* pales in comparison with the vast congregation halls of a gothic cathedral.

The front porch: Entrance to the *mandapa* is through the porch, sometimes called the *ardha-mandapa*. A big metal bell usually hangs from the ceiling of the porch. Devotees ring this bell to announce their arrival.

The reservoir: If the temple is not near a natural body of water, a reservoir of freshwater is built on the temple premises. The water is used for many purposes, including rituals and cleansing. Devotees use the water in the reservoir for a ritual bath before entering the temple.

The walkway: Most temples have a passage around the walls of the inner chamber for circumambulation by worshippers. This is commonly done as a mark of respect for the deity. Circumambulation is traditionally done clockwise. Each of the principal parts of a temple often is crowned by pyramidal towers. If that's the case, the heights are carefully graded so that the tallest tower corresponds to the *garbha-griha* and the shortest aligns with the porch.

Fascinating so far? If you are not excited by *garbha-grihas* and *gopuras*, my apologies for taking you through this temple architectural tour. Now let me return to the question I posed at the beginning. If you said the South Indian Ranganathaswamy Temple is the tallest, you are right—its *gopura* measures 73 meters and is the highest of the five. In fact Ranganathaswamy Temple is the tallest Hindu temple in the world. The *shikhara* of the original Sun Temple of Konark was 70 meters high

---

[28] Indian dances are invariably linked to Shiva, the lord of dance. We will discuss classical dances in book 5 of this series.

THE ASCENT OF VISHNU AND THE FALL OF BRAHMA

before it collapsed in 1628. The tallest tower of Angkor Wat, the world's largest Hindu temple in terms of land area, is 65 meters. The following table lists these temples in terms of height and land area.

Temple	Highest Shikhara/Gopura	Land Area (acres)
Trichy Ranganathaswamy	73 m (240 ft)	160
Sun Temple of Konark	70 m (229 ft)	11
Angkor Wat	65 m (213 ft)	500
Swaminarayan Akshardham	43 m (141 ft)	100
Khajuraho Kandariya Mahadeva	31 m (102 ft)	(part of a group of temples)

Now that you have some understanding of Hindu temples, we will explore a world-class temple in the next chapter.

19

Angkor Wat – The Mother of All Temples

I must confess Swaminarayan Akshardham Temple in Delhi, India is not like a typical Hindu temple that you may have visited. Built in 2005, this modern temple showcases Indian culture and heritage through a combination of architecture, exhibitions, gardens, a musical fountain, and even a boat ride. When I visited this temple in the winter of 2010, I was astounded by its size and smugly told myself that this must be the largest Hindu temple in India, if not the world. On a site of more than one 100 acres, the Akshardham Temple is indeed a colossal structure and a famous tourist attraction. But I was wrong. The largest Hindu temple in the world is the 800-year-old temple called Angkor Wat, often referred to as the mother of all temples.[29] Angkor Wat's 500 acres make Akshardham look small. Angkor Wat is not only the largest Hindu temple but the

---

[29] The largest Hindu temple in India, in terms of land size, is the Ranganathaswamy Temple located in Tamil Nadu, India. The Akshardham Temple is second but is often called the largest *comprehensive* Hindu temple.

largest of any religious monument in the world. The fact that the largest temple of the Hindus is located 5000 km away from India in a country called Cambodia has dented Hindu pride from time immemorial. After all, India—not Cambodia—is the birthplace of Hinduism and home to more than a billion Hindus.

About 18 times smaller than India, Cambodia has more than a thousand ancient temples. The best known is unquestionably Angkor Wat, and it has become a symbol of the country. In fact, the mere mention of Cambodia often brings Angkor Wat to mind. The temple appears on Cambodia's national flag and is the country's prime tourist attraction. For a country of 15 million people, Angkor Wat is so large in the public imagination that it embodies the entire civilization of Angkor, which was once the capital of the Khmer Empire and now is a city in modern-day Cambodia.

Panoramic view of Angkor Wat temple

How did the long arms of Hinduism reach Cambodia? Although modern Cambodia's population is 95 percent Buddhist, it wasn't always like this. In fact Hinduism, which is believed to have arrived in Cambodia during the reign of the Guptas, has deep roots there. Kings of Cambodia's Funan Kingdom (100 BCE–500 CE) worshipped Vishnu and Shiva. During the Khmer Empire (802–1431 CE) Cambodia was ruled by a series of Hindu kings. The pinnacle of Khmer architectural achievement, Angkor Wat, was built by the Khmer king Suryavarman II during his 36 years on the throne (1113–49 CE). Suryavarman's ascent to power was dramatic. When he was only fifteen, he leaped onto the head of the elephant on which the enemy king Harshavarman was riding and killed him instantly, an act often described as how "Garuda on a mountain ledge would kill a serpent." Suryavarman also is said to have later slain his great uncle Dharaindravarman I in a contest that lasted one day. After Suryavarman became monarch, he made several attacks on neighboring Vietnam to extend his territory. Although his bellicose policy continued throughout his rule, the king is also known to have initiated the first diplomatic overtures toward China.

Suryavarman died in combat, and we do not have not enough information about him to know whether he succeeded as either a warrior or a diplomat. However, his achievement as a builder of great monuments is beyond question. Suryavarman is credited with extending numerous temples during his reign and with creating the temples of Wat Athvea, Thommanon, Chau Say Tevoda, Banteay Samre, and Beng Maealea in addition to the jewel of Khmer architecture, Angkor Wat. These projects were not only numerous but massive, particularly Angkor Wat. The requirements for labor and material must have been especially challenging, given the temple's size. Building Angkor Wat is thought to have taken about 30 years in those days, whereas construction of the 21st century temple Akshardham took only five years.

Unlike most Angkorian temples, Angkor Wat is oriented toward the west, the direction of death in Hindu mythology, which led some scholars to conclude that Angkor Wat must have been primarily a tomb. This theory was supported by the fact that the bas-reliefs of the temple were designed to be viewed in an anticlockwise direction, a practice that has precedents in ancient Hindu funerary rites. The theory, however, all but ignored Vishnu's association with the direction of west. Suryavarman was a staunch devotee of Vishnu, and the name given to Suryavarman posthumously was Paramavishnuloka, which means "one who is the supreme abode of Vishnu." The temples created during his reign deviated from the Shaiva tradition and were devoted to Vishnu. Thus the themes of Angkor Wat, Wat Athvea, and Thommanon were predominantly Vaishnava, although Shaivite scenes also were represented—which also illustrates the liberal Khmer attitudes about religious beliefs. Wat Athvea also faces west. The temples of Thommanon and its twin, Chau Say Tevoda, have gateways that face both east and west. We will never know whether Suryavarman planned Angkor Wat as a temple or mausoleum, but he was never buried on the temple premises. He died in battle during a failed military expedition to conquer Vietnam.

The central tower of Angkor Wat is 65 meters high and is surrounded by four smaller towers with a series of enclosures, re-creating the image of Mount Meru, the mythical abode of the gods. A towering statue of Vishnu sits atop the central tower. Surrounding the temple is a moat whose perimeter is more than five kilometers and is the site of fevered boat races during the water festival. Visitors to Angkor Wat are struck not only by its imposing grandeur but by the extensive bas-reliefs. The narrative reliefs stretch a staggering 1.4 kilometers (nearly a mile) around the temple, and most scenes are from Hindu epics or mythology. They depict the Kurukshetra

Aerial view of Angkor Wat complex

Bas-reliefs of apsaras at Angkor Wat

War in the Mahabharata, the famous churning of the milky ocean, the victory of Vishnu over the *asuras*, the Battle of Lanka from the Ramayana, and many more. The temple is also famous for the more than 3,000 beguiling *apsaras* carved into its walls. The elegance of their postures and the thin sarongs clinging to their legs highlight the seductive qualities of these Cambodian *apsaras*, and their flowing garments, long sashes, rich jewelry, and unique hairstyles embody the native style.

Among the many depictions of Hindu gods in Angkor Wat are a few statues of Buddha. In fact one gallery is known as the Hall of Thousand Buddhas. Originally dedicated to Vishnu, Angkor Wat became a significant Buddhist pilgrimage site when Theravada Buddhism became the religion of Cambodia around the 14th century and has remained so ever since. The temple received more Buddhist additions in the 16th century.

A condensed list of large Hindu temples is provided at the end of this chapter. You can see the strikingly large land area of Angkor Wat compared to other temples. Although superlatives are inadequate to describe the glory of Angkor Wat, the fact that the largest Hindu temple is located outside India is unpalatable to many Hindus. So plans are afoot in India to build the world's largest Hindu temple in the style of Angkor Wat. Whether this temple will restore the centuries-old damage to the pride of Hindus only time will tell.

(My gratitude to Acharya Ram Sivan of the Australian Council of Hindu Clergy, New South Wales for sharing his expertise on Angkor Wat.)

List of Large Hindu temples

	Name	Land Area (acres)	Main Deity	Location
1	Angkor Wat	500	Vishnu/Buddhist	Angkor, Cambodia
2	Ranganathaswamy Temple	160	Vishnu	Trichy, Tamil Nadu, India
3	Swaminarayan Akshardham	100	Hindu pantheon	Delhi, India
4	Thillai Nataraja Temple	60	Shiva	Chidambaram, Tamil Nadu, India
5	Belur Math	40	Ramakrishna Paramahamsa	Kolkata, West Bengal, India
6	Annamalaiyar	25	Shiva	Thiruvannamalai, Tamil Nadu, India
7	Ekambareswarar	23	Shiva	Kanchipuram, Tamil Nadu, India
8	Jambukeswarar Temple	18	Shiva	Trichy, Tamil Nadu, India
9	Meenakshi Amman	17	Shiva	Madurai, Tamil Nadu, India
10	Vaitheeswaran Koil	15	Shiva	Tamil Nadu, India

✦ ✦ ✦

20

Exploring Mythology Through Paintings

Is art your cup of tea? Consider yourself lucky, if you enjoy dabbling in art, for art is not second nature to everyone. An old Hindu proverb says, "The man who knows nothing of music, literature, or art is no better than a beast, only without a beast's tail or teeth." In the course of its long history, India has had some uncultivated beasts in high places, and the most prominent among them was Aurangzeb, a 17th century Mughal ruler of India. Aurangzeb came from a rich artistic tradition yet had an utter disregard for art—particularly the non-Muslim variety—and went to great lengths to remove paintings from the walls of his royal court. The generations of artisans and painters living in his kingdom had to flee his wrath and take refuge in neighboring countries. Thankfully, Aurangzeb[30] was an exception. Throughout its history India was blessed with many

---

[30] Although Aurangzeb is considered one of the worst rulers of India, Pakistanis and conservative Muslims believe he is one of the greatest because he upheld Islamic traditions.

rulers of exceptional artistic sense, and this led to the creation of many cultural icons like Ajanta and Ellora, temples carved into hillside rock. The white marble tomb known as the Taj Mahal, one of the wonders of the world, was incidentally built by Aurangzeb's father, Shah Jahan.

The joys of art often remain a mystery to those who are less talented, but even artistic types have difficulty understanding and appreciating art, especially when the prerequisites have not been met. According to the Vishnudharmottara Purana, to appreciate art to the fullest, one must know dancing, music, and painting. Although the ancient text states the obvious, it makes a tacit assumption that you are familiar with the subject of artistic work. There's no point in gazing at an ancient Mewar painting that depicts the pastoral scenes of Krishna *lila* if the name Krishna is not familiar to you. But when you know Hindu mythology and stand in front of these pictures, they spring to life. The characters of the story will transport you to the bygone era of the gods. Until now we have been discussing literature that describes gods and their mythology. In this chapter we provide the background for looking at mythology from a different perspective: ancient paintings. These paintings open a window on traditional Indian cultures, although the view is often filtered by the sources.

The bright colors of Indian paintings, along with their minute details and highly exciting subjects like Krishna and Shiva, have always fascinated aficionados. These paintings came out of an artistic tradition that was almost entirely religious. The sculptural tradition of portraying gods as superhuman beings with multiple limbs also shows up in Indian painting, which depicts these divine figures in central roles in the elaborate mythologies of Hinduism, Buddhism, and Jainism. The artistic landscape changed with the arrival of outside cultural influences, especially from Muslim rulers, whose tastes were informed by the Middle East. Under their patronage Indian painting began to incorporate more worldly themes, such as the bravery of mortals, the intricacy of romantic love, or the pure delight of the senses. Soon artists were depicting Krishna as a cowherd and giving the emperors haloes. Thus in this new artistic paradigm gods became human and mortals divine.

EXPLORING MYTHOLOGY THROUGH PAINTINGS

The earliest paintings of ancient India are prehistoric rock paintings. These crude paintings, which are more than 10,000 years old, are found in many places, including the Bhimbetka[31] rock shelters in Madhya Pradesh. More formal Indian paintings generally are either wall paintings or miniatures. The wall paintings, or murals, are large works executed on solid structures in temples and palaces scattered throughout India. The earliest remnants of wall painting are in the Jogimara Caves of Madhya Pradesh, whereas the cave temples of Ajanta have the most extensive murals, which date to the fifth century CE.[32] Some show a hint of Hellenic influence in their use of perspective and three-quarter profiles. The Greek connection to India had its origins in the invasion of India by Alexander the Great about 200 years after Buddhism was born. The invasion opened up trade routes between India and the West that led to the exchange of cultural traditions.

Fresco (somewhat deteriorated) on a wall at Cave #2, Ajanta Caves, Maharashtra, India

---

[31] Bhimbetka was declared a UNESCO World Heritage Site in 2003.
[32] Ellora, Bagh, and Sittanavasal also have well-known murals.

THE ASCENT OF VISHNU AND THE FALL OF BRAHMA

Vrikshaka, a tree goddess, at an eighth-century Hindu temple

If you are familiar with Greek art, you will notice that Indian art is different. Greek art emphasizes the physical. The aesthetic ideal of the Greeks was a human endowed with a keen intellect, acute beauty, and beautiful body. Apollo was considered the quintessence of that perfection. From this ideal of human perfection, the Greeks created philosophy, science, and the arts. In India, on the other hand, a foundation of faith underpins both life and art. Every aspect of Indian life has a spiritual background of enduring value. Comparing Greek and Indian art, Sir John Marshall (1876–1958), the British archeologist, wrote, "Hellenistic art never took real and lasting hold upon India for the reason that the temperaments of two people were radically dissimilar … The vision of the Indian was bounded by the immortal rather than the mortal, by the infinite rather than the finite." That is why Indian art shows no muscular men flaunting their biceps and triceps. However, the tantric elements of Hinduism led to the depictions of stunning *apsaras* with hourglass figures—sometimes engaged in *maithuna*—in both paintings and sculpture.

Miniatures are often called manuscript paintings since they originally appeared as illustrations in manuscripts. Miniatures are works on paper or paper-like (palm leaf) materials, usually in a series, bound between leather or cardboard covers. Although murals date from second century BCE, most surviving miniatures are later than the 10th century CE. Early miniatures painted on wood and cloth did not withstand the ravages of time and were lost. Paper did not arrive on the subcontinent until the 12th or 13th century.

But nothing about miniature paintings is miniature. Most are bigger than the size of this book and therefore are miniature only in comparison with other forms of paintings. These paintings were originally created

Ganesha, Basholi miniature, ca. 1730

for kings and royal families by painters living under their patronage. The Palas of Bengal were the pioneers of miniature painting, and the art reached its glory during the Mughal period. As in sculpture,[33] India had several schools of miniature painters throughout its history. Some of the famous schools and their distinctive styles are described at the end of this chapter. Although the schools are based on regions and came to prominence at different times, a key characteristic—microscopic brushwork—is common in all genres of Indian painting. Indian painters used a subtle touch and extraordinary clarity of line to create minute details. In fact many aspects of Indian painting technique—from the selection of paintbrush hairs to the preparation of paper—were designed to facilitate such fine brushwork.

In the world of miniature paintings, signed works are rare. Importance was given to the work, not the painter, so most works remained unsigned. Several accounts, however, indicate that master artists were held in high esteem and richly rewarded. Miniature painting generally has enjoyed encouragement and patronage across all geographies, and this is reflected in the high quality of the paintings. The arrival of photography doomed miniature painting. As the traditional manuscript painter lost his royal patronage, only a few continued their profession into the 20th century.

Time and space do not allow us to further discuss murals and miniatures in this book, but we will pick up murals again in book 4 of this series when we discuss the Ajanta Caves. The next table lists the famous schools of miniature painting and the features of each. In this short treatment on paintings, we could not go into the details of works from important centers like Kangra, Basholi, Bundi and Tanjore. Later in this book, we'll describe a unique type of miniature painting, *ragamala*, that combines painting with music and poetry.

---

[33] As we discussed earlier, the Gandhara is a style of Buddhist visual art that developed between the first century BCE and the seventh century CE in India in what are today northwestern Pakistan and eastern Afghanistan. During the reign of Emperor Ashoka (third century BCE), this region was the site of intensive Buddhist missionary activity.

Famous Old Schools of Miniature Painting

Genre	Salient Features
Pre-Mughal	Earliest representations of Buddhist graphic symbols. Deities were designed by the Pala school of Bengal. Miniature painters followed the rules of mural paintings, but this style disappeared from India by the 12th century CE.
	Artists in the state of Gujarat developed miniature paintings of Vaishnavas and Jains in the 10th century CE. Subsequently Jain miniatures moved away from flat, two-dimensional compositions to animated, brightly colored paintings. Paintings often illustrated the text. The Jain paintings led to the formation of Gujarat School from where it spread to Rajasthan and Malwa (formerly a region of North India) and finally morphed into Rajput painting, which specialized in portraying events described in the epics.
Mughal	Paintings were Persian in style and included scenes of warfare, hunting, and trials of strength. The style was an amalgamation of Chinese and Central Asian art with Italian influence toward the end of the period. The paintings were meticulously detailed with heraldic characters. The emperors Akbar and Jahangir encouraged the illustration of epics and histories like the Ramayana, Mahabharata, Akbarnama, and Hamzanama. The style saw a return to naturalism and disregarded perspective and volume.
	The Deccan school marked the end of the Mughal school and was characterized by paintings that were rigid but decorative. They were more Indian than Persian
Rajput	Unlike the heraldic court style of the Mughal school, Rajput themes were flexible, and paintings depicted festivals and mythological subjects. The movement coincided with the spread of the cult of Krishna (bhakti movement) and depicted episodes from the life of Krishna. The Rajput school has two renowned branches: Rajasthani and Pahari.
Rajasthani	Important schools include Mewar, Marwar, and Bundi. Mewar stood out for its portrayal of Krishna, whereas Bundi was famous for brilliant colors and a nearly impressionist style. The Bihar school, which evolved at the end of the Rajasthani movement, produced paintings of Mughal influence with their characteristic attention to detail and use of heraldic characters.

Genre	Salient Features
Pahari	Also known as Punjab Hills. Important centers were Basholi, Jammu, and Kangra. The Pahari school was not only technically superior but lively and romantic.
Kangra	Romantic paintings that reached a crescendo in the depiction of Shiva and Krishna legends.
Tanjore	Originated in town of Thanjavur in Tamil Nadu. Most depicted scenes from Hindu epics and popular Hindu deities. They were usually panel paintings on wood planks.
Mysore	A new genre of painting inspired by the Vijayanagara tradition of South India. Like Tanjore, the Mysore themes were popular Hindu deities and scenes from Hindu epics.
Madhubani	An important school of folk painting practiced in the Mithila region of Bihar. Themes were Hindu deities and epic tales, especially of Krishna.
Pattachitra	Pattachitra means "cloth painting" and was popular in the state of Odisha. The style was later linked to the worship of Jagannath of Puri.

21

Andal – The Girl Who Ruled Over the Lord

Having produced more holy men and women than any other country, India is not only the land of spirituality but also the saint factory of the world. As the global leader in saint making, India has produced more saints per capita per century than any other culture in the world. At any point in time, the number of Hindu gurus, or swamis—as they are often called—exceeds the number of saints that Catholicism has recognized in its entire 2,000 year history. Indian saints come in many colors and stripes with the underlying message of inner bliss. In this chapter we profile one of the oldest South Indian Vaishnava saints, Andal.

Andal is believed to have lived between the fourth and ninth centuries. She was abandoned as a baby and found by a devout Brahmin called Periyalvar while hoeing basil in his garden. (Basil, or Tulsi, is sacred for Hindus.) Periyalvar had no family of his own and believed it was god's grace that gave him a child. He took her home and raised her as his own.

Andal grew up in an atmosphere of love and devotion, cared for by her doting father, who sang songs about Vishnu and shared his passion for Tamil poetry. From early childhood Andal could imagine no one other than Vishnu as her future husband. When her foster father prepared flower garlands as offerings to Vishnu at the local temple, Andal would secretly adorn herself with a garland, pretending she was a beautiful bride going to meet her divine groom. One day Periyalvar noticed a strand of hair on a garland and became suspicious. Much to his disappointment, he learned that Andal has desecrated the garland by wearing it. So he prepared another garland with pure flowers for his lord. (Hindu tradition holds that flowers should be pure and not be even smelled before being offered to a god.) That night Vishnu appeared before Periyalvar in a vision and asked him why he had discarded Andal's garland instead of offering it to him. For Vishnu the impure garland Andal had worn was more special than the pure garland Periyalvar offered. After that Periyalvar allowed Andal to play with the garlands as much as she wanted, for he realized that his child was true to her name—"the girl who ruled over the lord."

Andal later became more absorbed in her worship of Vishnu. As she was growing up, she composed two poetic works in devotion to Vishnu, *Tiruppavai* and *Nacciyar Tirumoli*. When Periyalvar started looking for a suitable husband for her, she refused marriage, because she wanted only to be a bride of Vishnu. Periyalvar, however, was more than happy to accommodate her wish. Because he did not know which form of Vishnu his daughter was obsessed with, Periyalvar recited songs to each of the manifestations of Vishnu by going to various places on foot. Andal responded to the song celebrating Ranganatha, the deity of Ranganathaswamy Temple (Trichy, Tamil Nadu) in the largest temple of India. Once again Vishnu appeared before Periyalvar in a vision and commanded him to present his bride to him for the wedding. When Andal arrived at the shrine, she blissfully approached the reclining image of Vishnu and merged with it, never to be seen again.

Andal was only 16 at that time and achieved in her short life what ordinary mortals take a lifetime to achieve. As one of the best-loved poet-saints of the Tamils, she was also the only woman in the group of twelve Alvars, the devotees of Vishnu responsible for revitalizing Hindu religious life. Her foster father, Periyalvar, was also an Alvar. The influence of her poetry on the daily religious life of South India has been phenomenal.

Both of Andal's short poems are included in the Tamil Vaishnava sacred texts and use Tamil motifs to praise Vishnu. Although Andal's chosen deity was Ranganatha, her poetry is dedicated to Krishna, a popular avatar of Vishnu. In the tradition of bridal mysticism, where the poet becomes the lover of a god, she frequently used the image of plunging herself into water to describe her desire for total immersion, and thus loss of self, in Krishna's grace. The *Tiruppavai*, a poem of thirty verses, contains verses of separation in which she mourns the absence of Krishna using the language and image of a forlorn lover. She portrays herself as a cowherd during the incarnation of Krishna and bemoans her jealousy of Krishna's conch because it enjoys the touch of his beautiful lips. *Tiruppavai* has become so popular in Tamil Nadu that it is recited every day for the entire month of Margali (December-January) to young girls seeking a husband. Like the Ramayana, people never get tired of listening to "Tiruppavai."

Fourteenth-century sculpture of Andal from Madurai, Tamil Nadu, India

Her longer work, *Nacciyar Tirumoli*, a poem of 143 verses, focuses in particular on Vishnu's forms as Krishna and Venkateswara. Like *Tiruppavai*, the *Nacciyar Tirumoli* achieved lasting fame. Sections of the text are recited at traditional weddings in Tamil Nadu even today, because "the girl who ruled over the lord" remains entrenched in Tamil religious life.

❃ ❃ ❃

22

Are You the Scientific Type?

For what a man would like to be true, that he more readily believes.

—FRANCIS BACON, 1561-1626

What type of person are you—the scientific type or the religious one? Whatever the types you and I are, there is something about our beliefs that defy rational explanation, according to late Professor Abraham Kovoor, psychiatrist and a leading rationalist of India. On his trip to Kolkata, India, Kovoor was asked by his neighbors in Kerala to bring them some sacred water from the Ganges, the holiest of rivers for the Hindus. At the Ganges, Kovoor found the water so muddy and polluted that he decided not to collect any for fear of making his neighbors ill. But he did not want to disappoint his neighbors, so Kovoor gave them some tap water and passed it off as sacred water. Months later he was surprised to learn that a neighbor had drunk the water and was completely cured of a severe bout of diarrhea. Another used it to fight flu and colds. The so-called sacred water also eased the labor pains of a third neighbor whose two previous childbirths had been complicated.

THE ASCENT OF VISHNU AND THE FALL OF BRAHMA

The Ganges meandering through the ranges at Rishikesh, Uttarakhand

I do not know what makes these devotees stick to their beliefs like cling-wrap. Most outsiders, after observing the sanctity of Hindu traditions like *muhurta*,[34] horoscopes, and *pujas*, conclude that Indians are

---

[34] *Muhurta* means "auspicious moment."

religious, conservative, and generally superstitious by nature. In the West, religion lost its place to science centuries ago. Just as people in the West believe in the authority of science without question, most Indians believe in the authority of their religion without question.

But if you think modern beliefs founded on science are infallible, think again. The original version of the Mudhadhiya Upanishad, one of oldest texts that dates to the fifth century CE, contains 108 verses of profound wisdom that, according to mythology, is accessible only to those who have reached a high level of spiritual attainment. The text is visible to Hindu saints, but when ordinary men and women look at it, its pages are blank. If I were to tell you that only a true *bhakta* can read it, on what grounds would you disagree? In fact for all I know, and for all you know, the fingerprints of god are visible only to his true devotees, those who constantly think about him.

Now, if a scientist were to confirm that the ink used to write this ancient text came from the ink sac of a pelagic octopus, and that the dried ink (containing the dye isopropyl zinthalyte) becomes visible only on days with a high UV index and only at certain places, such as those close to the equator, where there is less ozone to filter the sun's rays, we might all believe it—or not—for the ways of science, like the ways of god, are both magnificent and mysterious.

As humans we need to feel secure and be in control of things that concern us. Developing our own theories, explanations, and conclusions that make sense of our experiences is only natural. But whether it is science, religion, bhakti, astrology, or gut feeling, each of us will have confidence in something that we will never fully comprehend. This same confidence helps us to fight a cold or appreciate the marvel of invisible text. It is important that you realize this.

Before you turn to the next chapter, please be informed that there is no such thing as isopropyl zinthalyte. This empirical experiment was designed to illustrate the irrationality of our beliefs, whether they come from science or mythology. The scientific explanation about the effect of high UV on the ink's visibility was bunkum. Sorry! As a religious person,

THE ASCENT OF VISHNU AND THE FALL OF BRAHMA

if you think this is a fitting rebuke to scientists and rationalists for their unwavering faith in science, I am afraid this is not that proud moment. The Mudhadhiya (fools) Upanishad is never known to exist either.

> *In real life, [Diane] Keaton believes in God. But she also believes that the radio works, because there are tiny people inside it.*
>
> —WOODY ALLEN 1937-

23

Ragamala – A Garland of Melodies

> *Music gives a soul to the universe, wings to the mind, flight to the imagination and life to everything.*
>
> —PLATO

The transformative power of classical music can be observed by performing a simple experiment on the piano. Play the notes B and C a few times. If you listen carefully, the correlation between the two notes soon becomes clear: the job of C is to make B sad. Composers know this relationship, for if they want sad music, they play these two notes. Ancient Indians knew it, too. They observed that certain notes in a sequence evoked a certain mood—like sorrow or joy—in the listener. They used these notes to write a set of ragas (patterns of musical notes), then combined these ragas with paintings and poetry to create a literary trifecta known as *ragamala*, which means "garland of ragas."

A *ragamala* is a set of miniature paintings that depict various modes of Indian classical music. Each miniature illustrates a poem that attempts to evoke the mood of a particular raga. The poems are written across the top or on the reverse side of the painting and constitute the background music for viewing these pictures. The ragas also indicate the season and the time of the day when they are to be performed.[35] Many variations of *ragamala* exist, and their iconographies differ according to the regions and the times in which the *ragamalas* were created. Thus the iconography of a 19th century Mysore *ragamala* will be different from that of a Pahari or Rajasthani *ragamala* of the same period. Despite these variations, the emotive content associated with each raga has remained more or less constant across the years.

If you think you can stare at a *ragamala* painting and marvel at the art, you will be bitterly disappointed. Ancient Indian texts sometimes refer to a quality or experience called *rasa*,[36] or essence. It denotes the mood evoked by the artist. Old texts prescribe nine such moods called *navarasa*. For the quintessential *rasa* experience, both the artist and the audience should be proficient in the language of *rasa*. The audience should not only be trained in the art but also have a cultured palette that distinguishes the certain tones that conjure a sense of melancholy from those that signify euphoria. The ideal audience consists of *rasikas*, connoisseurs trained in the sensibility of *rasa*. These rasikas are not the genteel types who will soak up the artistic atmosphere silently without uttering a sound. Rather, the wowed rasikas of Indian art are often known to express their appreciation by gestures and making contented noises.

Ragamalas are one of the most popular genres of North Indian and Deccani paintings. They were less popular in the South, except in the state of Andhra Pradesh. Although the Mughals of the 16th century are credited with bringing a new dimension into Indian painting, *ragamala* paintings were known even before the Mughal period. They usually were

---

[35] Many Hindustani (northern Indian) ragas are prescribed for a particular time of the day or season. However, Carnatic (southern Indian) ragas do not have any such requirements.

[36] The concept of *rasa* is fundamental to many forms of Indian art, including dance, music, cinema, and literature.

Bhairavi ragini, Mughal style painting ca. 17th century, Bilaspur, Himachal Pradesh

presented in loose paper folios and were especially popular during the 15th century, when they were commissioned by rulers and noblemen. The most famous set was completed between 1640 and 1680 and adorns the

THE ASCENT OF VISHNU AND THE FALL OF BRAHMA

Ragamala Painting of raga (ragini) Todi (ca. 18th century, Kangra)

walls at the maharaja's palace in Bundi, Rajasthan. *Ragamalas'* popularity waned in the 19th century when royal patronage was no longer available.

Many ragas were used in *ragamala* paintings, and the popular ones include Megha, Bhairava, Shri, Hindola, and Deepak. Shiva is often associated with the Bhairava raga, whereas Mega is identified with Vishnu or sometimes Krishna. Over time music theorists categorized the numerous ragas in family groups, usually led by a patriarch raga, accompanied by *raginis* (wives) or by *ragaputras* (sons).[37] Thus the Hindola raga has Madhumadhavi as *ragini* and Vinoda as *ragaputra*. Although it may seem counterintuitive, a *raga* is not necessarily represented by a male figure nor a *ragini* by a female. The central figures of earlier *ragamalas* were mostly deities, but they were replaced by human beings by the middle of the 16th century. As the bhakti movement swept through India, one god in particular, Krishna, became the focus of North Indian devotion. The touching verses in praise of Krishna by the poet Mira Bai and the saint Surdas's alluring poems celebrating Krishna's childhood and adolescence were significant influences that changed the very essence of *ragamala* paintings.

The most popular subject of *ragamala* paintings was undoubtedly romance. In the *ragamala* painting from Kangra, Rajasthan, illustrated above, the raga mentioned is the lonely and lovelorn Todi.[38] The central character in Todi is always depicted as a woman who has ventured into the forest to meet her lover at a secluded spot. Typical descriptions of the scene suggest the lover is late and the woman is lonely in the woods, passing her time by playing a stringed instrument, with her anxiety building every moment he fails to appear. This well-known raga was the dominant theme of the famous Hindi film song "Raina Beeti Jaaye," widely regarded

---

[37] The *raga-ragini* classification system was used from the 14th until the 19th century. This scheme is no longer popular because of inconsistencies.

[38] Hindustani and Carnatic music are often accused of being false friends because the Hindustani *ragas* bear little resemblance to their counterparts in Carnatic. For example, the Todi *raga* of Hindustani classical music is entirely different from the Todi of Carnatic music.

THE ASCENT OF VISHNU AND THE FALL OF BRAHMA

as one of the finest classical solos of the 1970s.[39] Even after several centuries of devotional attention, Krishna is still the subject of the song, as these lines illustrate:

Raina Beeti Jaaye Shyam na aaye
  (The night is passing, but Krishna does not come)
Nindiya na aaye (Sleep does not come)
Raina Beeti Jaaye (The night is passing)
Shyam ko bhula Shyam ka vaada (Krishna forgot his promise)
Sang diye ki jage radha (Radha sits with her lamp, waiting for him)
...

...

Although *ragamala* paintings were in vogue until the 19th century, many questions still remain unanswered. First, it is not clearly understood how patrons used these paintings. They probably were used either for entertainment or for their educational value. In any case the subject matter offered artists an opportunity to display their talent, as they reinterpreted well-known themes in the most dramatic manner possible. Second, the true relationship of *ragamala* paintings and music remains elusive, not least because there were no recordings of musical performances before the 20th century. Furthermore, written musical notation arrived only recently in Indian music. Painters were not musicians and vice versa. As a result many Indian classical music experts dismiss the images and accompanying poetry because they believe they fail to capture the nuances of the music. However, no one disputes that this genre was one of the most popular and enduring among Rajput patrons and others. *Ragamala*s are perhaps the crude precursors of our modern-day music videos.

---

[39] The song was from the movie *Amar Prem* (1972) and was sung by the famous Indian playback singer Lata Mangeshkar.

24

Mira Bai – The Princess Who Became a Saint

> *The path of devotion, what in India is called bhakti yoga, the path of love and devotion—a Meera, a Chaitanya, dancing and singing, losing themselves completely in the act. When Meera is dancing there is only dance, there is no Meera; the dancer is completely merged into the dance. When Chaitanya is singing and dancing there is no Chaitanya; he has become one with the act.*
>
> —RAJNEESH, 1931-1990

In bridal mysticism the soul is the bride and the lord is the eternal groom. The mystic prepares for an intimate union, awaiting her deity's sacred touch as if it were the caress of her lover. But her deity's presence cannot be demanded, for divine union is not a matter of insistence. Instead the mystic must wait patiently in a state of utter devotion until that moment arrives. Salvation is attained by merging the soul with the deity, as did Andal, the seventh-century exponent of bridal mysticism.

The greatest among the female Indian saints, however, was Mira Bai, a poet who lived in the 16th century. If Andal was the queen of bridal mysticism, then Mira Bai was the empress. Andal and Mira Bai lived in different eras, grew up in different regions (South and North), and wrote poetry in their local languages (Tamil and Rajasthani). Although they were separated by distance, time, language, and culture, these Vaishnava *bhaktas* were united in their unflinching loyalty to their chosen deities.

Mira, sometimes spelled *Meera*, was a Rajput princess born in 1498 in a village called Merta in Northwest India. The "Bai" in her name came later as it was an honorific title attached to a woman's name. She came from a family of esteemed Rajput rulers known for their dignity and gallantry. Her great-grandfather founded the city of Jodhpur, and her grandfather defeated the advancing Mughals in many battles. Such was the valor of the Rajputs that if they were defeated in battle, their wives committed suicide en masse to avoid falling into the hands of the enemy. Mira lived during a period of great unrest—Muslim forces were invading North India, and the resident Hindus were struggling to preserve their livelihood and culture. Surrounded as they were by the growing influence of the Muslims, the Rajputs steadfastly maintained their tradition of martial valor and family honor.

Mira's family members were staunch devotees of Vishnu. According to legend, the five-year-old Mira, after watching a wedding procession, asked her mother who would become her future husband. Mira's mother took her into their home shrine and pointed to Krishna. Although the mother was not serious, her gesture marked the beginning of Mira's association with Krishna. After her mother died, Mira's father became preoccupied with the responsibilities of war and left Mira in the custody of her grandparents. The little girl was schooled at home, where she also was trained in music. The simplicity of her songs, and in later years her thorough mastery of the ragas, is often attributed to her early foundation in music.

While she was living with her grandparents, a significant event took place that would change Mira's life. A wandering mendicant who was carrying a statue of Krishna visited their home. Mira was instantly enamored

Painting of Mira Bai, artist unknown

with the statue and became inconsolable when he left. Legend has it that the mendicant had a vision in which he was told to return to the house and give the statue to the little girl. Thus began Mira's worship of the statue. She is said to have kept the statue with her until her last breath.

When Mira was 18, she was given in marriage to Bhoj Raj, the crown prince of Mewar, the most powerful Rajput state in the early 16th century.

Marriage may be a mosaic of small beautiful moments with your spouse, but for Mira these moments were full of conflict. It is said that on her wedding day, she performed the marriage rituals with the statue before performing them with her husband. And after marriage she refused to worship Durga, the chosen deity of her husband's family, and considered Krishna her divine match. After five years Bhoj Raj died of battle wounds, and Mira refused to join him on his funeral pyre in the ancient practice of sati. In doing so she was flouting tradition and disregarding the expectations of her in-laws. With the death of her husband, Mira's devotional practices became more intense. She sang and danced into ecstasies in public places, often with men and women of lower caste, a behavior deemed unbecoming of an aristocrat. Mira soon attracted a long list of devotees and a few fierce enemies: her in-laws.

Shocked by her actions, her in-laws locked her in the house. According to legend, several attempts were made on her life. In one tale someone sent Mira a basket of flowers with a poisonous snake hidden inside. But when Mira took the basket, the snake turned into a figurine of Vishnu. In another instance her husband's family exhorted Mira to drink a cup of poison, but the poison turned into nectar. According to another tale, her enemies tried to drown her in a river, but her body would not sink and remained floating. In still another tale the princess was forced to lie on a bed of nails, but the nails turned into flowers. Devotees of Mira believe that the miraculous escapes attributed to her were the result of divine intervention by Krishna, the reward for her fervent bhakti.

Weary of family machinations, Mira eventually left Mewar and retreated to her childhood home of Merta, where she faced more harassment, this time by an uncle who had ascended the throne after her father died in battle. Like many others, her uncle objected to her public displays of religious affections. Mira soon fled Merta and traveled to Vrindavan, where she joined a religious community. (Incidentally Vrindavan is where Krishna performed the famous dance *Rasa lila*[40] with the *gopis*,

---

[40] The *Rasa lila* is described in detail in book 4 of this series.

or cowherds.) Family honor no longer mattered to Mira. Like a helium balloon let loose, she wandered wherever she liked and danced with bells on her ankles and castanets in her hands. She spent an entire decade as a wandering mendicant before finally moving to Dwarka—another place with deep connections to the god Krishna—and died there in 1547.

There are many stories surrounding Mira's death. In one, Mira's in-laws sent a group of Brahmins to persuade her to come back to Mewar, but when Mira refused they threatened to fast until they died. Because she did not want to be responsible for their deaths, Mira headed to a temple of Krishna where she merged with the image of her lord, never to be seen again.

Did you find Mira's tale intriguing so far? I am afraid that most of Mira's story should be taken with a grain of salt. Details of her life are obscured by legend. Since there are no authentic records, stories about her remain controversial. Although manuscripts existed in Mira's day, preserving them was all but impossible. Another legend of contestable authenticity involves her meeting with Emperor Akbar, one of the greatest rulers India ever produced. This tale says that Akbar, a man of egalitarian tastes, was so enamored with her soulful music and devotional singing that he traveled from afar and disguised himself as a beggar so he could meet her. It is said that he placed a priceless necklace at Mira's feet before he left.

Although more than a thousand verses have been attributed to Mira, most scholars believe she composed somewhere between 100 and 200 verses, most while she was a wandering mendicant in Vrindavan. In her poems she expresses her longing for union with Krishna. At times she describes the joy of divine union and at other times the pain of separation.

I am longing for you, Oh my Lord,
For the season of swing has come,
But you are not beside me.
Clouds gather on my brows
And my eyes shed heavy shadows

THE ASCENT OF VISHNU AND THE FALL OF BRAHMA

My parents gave me to you,
I have become yours forever:
who but you can be my Lord?
The separation troubles my heart
Make me your own; Make me perfect like you,
O Lord of Perfection

Look, how he wounds me again
He vowed to come and the yard is empty,
flood flung away, like my senses
Why must you shame what you say?
You've wisped yourself away,
lifter of the mountain, left me here to splinter.

As one of the earliest poets Mira Bai still lives in the hearts of many people through her songs. Her songs are sung all over India. Although she lived during a period of war and spiritual decline, her life offered a shining example of pure devotion. She became a role model not only for her bhakti but for her fearless disregard for social and family conventions. She was also an inspiration to Gandhi because of her simplicity and non-violent resistance. Today the name Mira has become synonymous with the courage to stand up for what you believe. She has been the subject of many movies, paintings, and countless stories.

In musical circles Mira Bai is credited with creating the Hindustani raga known as "Mira's Malhar," a variation of an old Malhar raga.

> *With my tears, I watered the creeper of love that I planted;*
> *Now the creeper has grown spread all over, and borne the fruit of bliss.*
>
> —MIRA BAI, 1498-1547

❋ ❋ ❋

25

Devotion is Superior to Erudition

> *To succeed in your mission, you must have single-minded devotion to your goal.*
>
> —A. P. J. ABDUL KALAM, 1931-2015

Commonly defined as religious devotion, bhakti is a key concept in Hinduism that has withstood the test of centuries. It is the intense love of a devotee for a personal god and manifests in the devotee as a kind of divine-inspired madness and total indifference to worldly affairs. Bhakti's close relative, *vibhakti*, on the other hand, means "scholarship," particularly in religious matters, in a few vernacular Indian languages. The spiritually inclined are often curious to know whether bhakti or *vibhakti* is superior in the eyes of their god. The answer is almost always "it depends," for nothing can be taken for granted in Hinduism, not even karma. But Vaishnavas do have a definite preference, as the story of Poonthanam shows.

Poonthanam was born into a Brahmin family of Kerala in 1547 and married at the early age of twenty. He and his wife were childless for a long time. By regularly chanting the Santhana Gopala hymn, he appeased Krishna, the presiding deity at the temple of Guruvayur, and soon was blessed with a son.[41] Six months after the baby's birth, a ceremony for his first rice meal was arranged at his house. Many Brahmin families gathered for the occasion; women wore their customary white clothes and held palm leaf umbrellas. Once they were inside the house, the women put their cloth bundles in a corner of a room without realizing that the baby was sleeping there. When the time arrived for the start of the ceremony, the mother found that the baby had died of suffocation.

The grief-stricken Poonthanam sought refuge at Guruvayur and prostrated himself at Krishna's feet. Poonthanam lost interest in food and family. He spent his time reading the Bhagavata Purana, a classic that describes the life and times of Krishna, and translating hymns in praise of the lord in Malayalam, the only language Poonthanam knew.

Legend has it that he was consoled by Guruvayurappan himself (Krishna, the chief deity of Guruvayur Temple) who lay down on his lap as a child. In his devotional poetry entitled *Jnanappana*, Poonthanam ponders, "When little Krishna is playing in my mind, do I need another child of my own?

While Poonthanam was composing the *Jnanappana*, a Brahmin by the name of Melpathur Bhattathiri was among the throngs of devotees at Guruvayur. A learned Sanskrit scholar, he was intimately attached to his guru in the *guru-shishya* tradition of Hinduism. It is said that when his guru was bothered by rheumatism, Melpathur contracted the ailment himself as *guru-dakshina* (tuition fees). But he suffered so much from the disease that he began looking for a remedy. A well-known poet of those times, Ezhuthachan, directed Melpathur to Guruvayur, telling him to "start with fish." At first the advice sounded vague, if not offensive, for eating fish was taboo for the Brahmins. But Melpathur understood what the guru meant and began composing his famous work, *Narayaneeyam*,

---

[41] Santhana Gopala *stotra* is a prayer in the Bhagavata Purana that addresses young Krishna and is chanted by those seeking to conceive a child or have a safe pregnancy.

in which he describes the ten avatars of Vishnu, beginning with the fish avatar. Written in Sanskrit, *Narayaneeyam* is a summary of the Bhagavata Purana, except that at the end of every chapter the author makes an impassioned plea to his deity to cure him of his disease so that he can focus entirely on the greatness of his lord. His plea did not go unanswered—Melpathur was miraculously cured on the day he finished his composition.

While Poonthanam was at Guruvayur, he learned that Melpathur was in the temple composing his work. Poonthanam knew very little Sanskrit, yet he hastened to meet the renowned poet-scholar. However, he soon realized that Melpathur was not only erudite but extremely conceited. One day, during a discourse held at the Guruvayur Temple, Poonthanam incorrectly translated the words *Padmanabha Maraprabhu* as "Vishu, Lord of the trees." At once Melpathur openly mocked Poonthanam by saying, "Padmanabha is not lord of trees (Maraprabhu) but lord of immortals (Amaraprabhu)."

Like a true devotee, Poonthanam did not take the snub personally and concentrated on translating the Santhana Gopala story of the Bhagavata Purana from Sanskrit to Malayalam. After he completed the work, Poonthanam wanted someone to review what he had done. So he approached Melpathur, even though his contempt for average scholars was well known. Melpathur immediately snubbed Poonthanam by saying, "I don't see any point in reviewing this work. It will be teeming with mistakes befitting your ignorance of the language. My time is precious and not to be wasted in reviewing trivial work. Please take this work to someone else."

Needless to say, Poonthanam was crestfallen. He knew the translation was not perfect, but he had not anticipated an outright rejection. It was like losing another child. That night Melpathur could hardly sleep because the rheumatic fever had returned. Later that night he had a divine revelation in which Krishna appeared before him and said, "Your scholarship is indeed commendable, but I prefer the bhakti of Poonthanam to your *vibhakti*." Melpathur was completely shaken and could not get any sleep that night. He waited for dawn and rushed to meet Poonthanam. Melpathur apologized profusely to Poonthanam and gladly agreed to review the book.

Despite the return of his rheumatic fever, Melpathur produced outstanding religious literature during his lifetime. His Narayaneeyam occupies a lofty place in Sanskrit literature not only for its devotional fervor but for its literary merit. Yet the scholarship of Melpathur was overshadowed by the devotion of an ordinary man known only by his family name, Poonthanam, for no one knew his first name. Even though both worked on the Bhagavata Purana, the verses of Poonthanam's *Jnanappana*, starting with "Krishna, Krishna, Mukunda …" and written in the language of the masses, are today known to every Hindu family in Kerala. It is often referred to as the Bhagavad Gita, or the "song of wisdom," in his local language of Malayalam.

Painting of Poonthanam, artist unknown

> *Krishna, Krishna, Mukunda, Janardhana*
> *Krishna, Govinda, Narayana, Hare,*
> *Achuthananda, Govinda, Madhava,*
> *Sachidiananda, Narayana, Hare*

(Verses from Poonthanam's Jnanappana)

The pen may be mightier than the sword, but the story of Poonthanam reveals that the heart of the devotee is more precious than the ink of the scholar. This story conveys the essence of Vaishnava philosophy. While Shaivites prefer meditation and Advaitas prefer erudition, the emphasis for Vaishnavas has always been bhakti. For them nothing is more blissful than the joy that arises in the company of a god.

DEVOTION IS SUPERIOR TO ERUDITION

A little philosophy inclineth man's mind to atheism, but depth in philosophy bringeth men's minds about to religion.

–FRANCIS BACON, 1561-1626

26

Char Dham Yatra – A Pilgrimage of a Lifetime

Life is a pilgrimage. The wise man does not rest by the roadside inns. He marches direct to the illimitable domain of eternal bliss, his ultimate destination.

–SWAMI SIVANANDA, 1887-1963

For seekers of tranquility and spirituality, India is the ultimate destination. As the birthplace of several world religions, the Indian subcontinent is home to countless sacred and holy sites. A religious journey to these sacred places is a long-standing tradition of Hinduism. Every year many people from India and abroad embark on a pilgrimage influenced by their heritage or spiritual beliefs and sometimes as religious tourism. One of the most sacred routes for Hindus is the Char Dham *yatra* ("four temples trip"), which consists of visiting the four pilgrimage sites of Puri, Rameswaram, Dwarka, and Badrinath.

For Hindus the purpose of a pilgrimage is to accrue good karma and wash away the bad karma of the past. A trip to the Char Dham is considered highly sacred. Hindus believe every devotee should undertake the journey at least once in their lifetime. Yet a Char Dham pilgrimage can become an ordeal in travel because the four holy sites are located at the four corners of the vast country.

Although the origins of the Char Dham pilgrimage remain obscure, it is generally believed that the eighth-century reformer and philosopher Shankara coined the term *Char Dham* by grouping the four important holy places. Badrinath is in the northern part of India in the state of Uttarakhand. Located deep within the Himalayas, the Badrinath Temple is considered the seat of Vishnu in his aspect of Badrinarayan. It is by far the most important temple and receives more visitors than any of the three other shrines. Rameswaram is in the southern state of Tamil Nadu and gains its significance from the Ramayana. At the Ramanathaswamy Temple in Rameswaram, Rama is said to have built a *linga* (column of light) and worshipped it to get the blessings of Shiva before waging war against the demon king Ravana.

Sites of Char Dham pilgrimage

The eastern state of Odisha is home to the city of Puri, which is famous for the ancient temple Jagannath Puri. The presiding deity is Krishna, who is celebrated as Lord Jagannath. The famous Hindu saint Chaitanya, the inspiration for the Hare Krishna movement, is believed to have merged with the statue of Jagannath in this temple. Ironically Hare Krishnas are not allowed to enter this temple, which still upholds the tradition of allowing entry only to true blue Hindus. Dwarka, an ancient city of historic and religious importance to Hindus, is in the western part of India, in the state of Gujarat.

As you may realize, the Char Dham has particular appeal for Vaishnavas because three of the four sites are associated with Vishnu and only one with Shiva. Although the name Rameswaram suggests a Vaishnava connection, the Ramanathaswamy Temple in Rameswaram[42] is a Shiva temple and perhaps the most beautiful of the shrines of the Char Dham sites.

When Hindus talk about Char Dham, they include the alternate sites of Yamunotri, Gangotri, Kedernath, and Badrinath, all of which are located in the Himalayas in the state of Uttarakhand. Originally this Himalayan pilgrimage route was dubbed the Chota (little) Char Dham, but over the years it became synonymous with Char Dham even though discerning devotees maintain the distinction by calling it the Himalayan Char Dham. In the past making a pilgrimage to the Himalayan Char Dham was treacherous, but improvements in infrastructure have made access easier for devotees. Unlike the original Char Dham, the sites of the Himalayan Char Dham represent the three major sects of Hinduism: Badrinath is Vaishnava, Kedernath is Shaiva, and Gangotri and Yamunotri are both Devi sites.

Sites of Himalayan Char Dham pilgrimage

For pilgrims the Himalayan Char Dham is more practical because the sites are relatively close to each other. More than 250,000 devotees make the Himalayan journey each year.

---

[42] Rameswaram means "the god worshipped by Rama."

THE ASCENT OF VISHNU AND THE FALL OF BRAHMA

*Faith is not the clinging to a shrine but
an endless pilgrimage of the heart.*

–ABRAHAM JOSHUA HESCHEL, 1907-1972

Index

A

Abraham · 5, 10
Adam · 19
Adi Parashakti · 23
Advaita Vedanta · 24, 61
Agni · 22, 24, 67, 74
Airavata · 32
Ajanta Caves · 98-99, 102
Akbar · 55, 103, 123
Akbarnama · 103
Alexander the Great · **47-49**, 52, 54, 99
Ali, Muhammad · 39
Allen, Woody · 112
Alvar · **69-70**, 80, 81, 106, 107
Amar Prem (movie) · 118
Amarnath · 74
amrita · 29-30, 32-34
Amritanandamayi · 24
Ananda Sayana · **29**, 44, 55, 78
Ananda Shesha · 2, 44, 75
Andal · 69, 81, **105-107**, 119-120
Angkor Wat · 8, 81, 87, 90, **91-96**
Annamalaiyar · 96
Anushasana Parva · 60
Apollo · 100
Appar · 69

apsara · 32, 84, 95, 100
ardha-mandapa · 89
Arjuna · 59, 65
Aryaman · 22
Ashoka Chakra · 54
Ashoka Maurya (Ashoka) · 54-55, 102
asura · 11, 19, 31, 33-34, 95
atman · 27, 61, 80
Aurangzeb · 76, 97-98

B

Bacon, Francis · 109, 129
Badrinarayan · 132
Badrinath · 131-133
Bagh · 99
Bai, Mira · 68, 70, 81, 117, **119-124**
Bamiyan Buddha · 47, 49
Banteay Samre · 93
Basava · 69
Basholi · 102, 104
beginning of the world · **1-4**
Belur Math · 96
Beng Maealea · 93
Bhagavad Gita · 53, 59, 62, 68, 70-71, 79, 128
bhajan · 61, 81

bhakta · 41, 68, 111, 120
bhakti · 43, **67-71**, 79-80, 103, 111, 117, 119, 122, 124-125, 127-128
bhang · 67
Bhattar, Parasara · 61
Bhattathiri, Melpathur · 68, **126**
bhava · 79
Bhimbetka · 99
Bhishma · 59, 61
Bhrigu · 39, 40
boar · 8, 36
boon of conditional immortality · 8
Brahma · 2-3, **5-15**, 18-19, 21, 23-25, 27, 35-37, 39-40, 74, 83, 86
Brahman · 6, 21, 23-24, **25-27**, 45, 61, 68, 80
  Nirguna · 26
  Saguna · 26, 68
Brahmani · 7
Brahmin · 5, 25, 27, 52-53, 55, 77, 105, 123, 125-126
bridal mysticism · 68-69, 81, 107, **119-120**
Buddha · 47, 49, 52, 74, 95
Buddhism · 47, 51, 54-57, 69, 95, 98-99
  Mahayana · 56
  Theravada · 95
Buddhist · 48
Bundi · 102-103, 117
Burma (Myanmar) · 5

C

Cambodia · 8, 81, 87, 92, 95-96
Campbell, Joseph · 10
Carnatic music · 1, 70, 114, 117
Carter, Jimmy · 49
Chaitanya · 70, 80-81, 119, 132
Chandra · 55, 77
Chandra Gupta · 55
Chandragupta Maurya · 54-55
Char Dham · 76, **131-133**
Chau Say Tevoda · 93, 94
Chota Char Dham · **133**
churning of the milky ocean · 14, **29-34**, 95
classical music · 1, 113, 117-118
Coomaraswamy, Ananda · 51

D

Dalai Lama · 57, 78
Damodara · 61
Das, Tulsi · 70, 81
Dasa, Purandara · 70
Dashavatara · 54, 57
Deccani painting · 114
Deogarh · 55
deva · 11, 13, 19
Devi · 6, 23-24, 62, 77, 133
Dhanavantari · 32-33
Dharaindravarman · 93
dharma · 12, 42, 52-53, 59, 61, 85

Dharmashastra · 52
Dharmasutra · 52
Dhruva · **63-65**, 83
Dnyaneshwar · 70
Dravida · 88
Durga · 24, 53, 122
Durvasa · 29, 30
Dvaita · 61
Dwarka · 123, 131-132

E

Ekambareswarar · 96
Elephanta caves · 23
Ellora Caves · 98-99
Emerson, Ralph Waldo · 1
Erawan Shrine of Bangkok · 8
Ezhuthachan · 126

F

Franklin, Benjamin · 73
Funan Kingdom · 92

G

Gandhara · 47-49, 102
Ganesha · 24, 62, 75, 77
Ganges · 109
Gangotri · 133
garbha-griha · **88-89**

Garuda · 44, 60, 93
Gaudiya sect · 80
Gayatri · 7
Gita Govinda · 79
Gopala · 61, 126
gopi · 122
gopura · 88-89
Great Deluge · 17
Grousset, Rene · 23
gurdwara · 74
Guru Granth Sahib · 74
Guru Nanak · 74
guru-dakshina · 69, 126
Guruvayur · 126-127

H

Halahala · 32
Hall of Thousand Buddhas · 95
hamsa · 9
Hamzanama · 103
Hanuman · 65
Hari · 34, 44, 85, 86
Harihara · 23, 62
Harivamsa · 53
Harshavarman · 93
Heschel, Abraham Joshua · 134
Himalayan Char Dham · **133**
Hindu · 3-4, 7, 12, 18, 21, 24-26, 48, 71, 75-77, 92, 96, 105, 109, 120, 131-133
Hindu Kush · 48

Hinduism · 2-3, 9, 11, 14, 23-24, 26-27, 35, 39, **51-52**, 55-57, 60-61, 65, 68-69, 75, 79, 92, 98, 100, 125-126, 131, 133
Hindustani music · 1, 114, 117, 124
Hiranyagarbha · 8
Hiranyakashipu · 43
Holi · 67
Holkar, Ahilya Bai · 76

I

Iliad · 53
India · 1, 5, 19, 23, 47-49, 51-56, 59, 61, 67-71, 73-78, 80-81, 88, 91-92, 96-97, 99-100, 102-107, 109, 117, 119-120, 123-124, 131-133
Indra · 10, 13-14, 22, 24, 29-30, 32, 43, 65, 67, 84
Islam · 1, 25, 47, 49, 71, 73, 77, 97

J

Jagannath · 76, 81, 104, 132
Jagannath Temple · 76, 81
Jain · 48, 103
Jainism · 47, 51, 98
Jambukeswarar Temple · 96
Jaya · 42
Jnanadeva · 70
Jnanappana · 126, 128

Jnaneshwar · 70
Jogimara Caves · 99
Jyotirlinga · 77

K

Kailash · 40, 75, 84
Kalam, Abdul · 125
Kalidasa · 23
kalpa · **11-13**, 18
Kama · 84-85
Kamadhenu · 32
Kangra · 102, 104, 117
Kanja · 8
Kanyakumari · 74
karma · 27, 125, 132
Kashi Vishwanath Temple · 76
Kaurava · 59
Kaustubha · 32, 44
Kedernath · 133
Ketu · 33
Khajuraho Kandariya Mahadeva Temple · 87, 90
Khmer Empire · 92-94
Kondabolu, Hari · 34
Kovoor, Abraham · 109
Kripa · 49
Krishna · 8, 17, 25-26, 32, 37, 43, 53, 59, 68, 70, 75-76, 79-81, 98, 103-104, 107, 117-118, 120, 122-123, 126-128, 132
Kshatriya · 52

Kuchela · 17, 83
Kurukshetra War · 53

L

Lakshmi · 1-3, 32, 40, 44, 53, 75, 77, 80, 84, 86
linga · 36, 74, 132
Linga of Light · 37

M

Madhava · 61, 80, 128
Madhubani painting · 104
Mahabharata · 13, 29, 43, 53-54, 59, 60, 62, 65, 70, 95, 103
mahadeva · 21, 56, 87, 90
maha-pralaya · 11
Mahatma Gandhi · 81
maha-yuga · **12-13**
maithuna · 100
Malwa painting · 103
manasaputra · 19
mandapa · 89
Mangeshkar, Lata · 118
Manikkavachakar · 69
Manu · 13-14, **17-19**, 52, 60, 63, 68
Manusmriti · 19, 52
manvantara · **13-14**, 18-19
marijuana · 67
Markandeya (sage) · 13
Marwar painting · 103

Matsya avatar · 19
Maya · 6
Meenakshi · 78, 96
Meenakshi Amman Temple · 78
Mehta, Narsi · 81
Menaka · 32
Merta · 120, 122
Mewar painting · 98, 103
miniature painting · **100-103**, 113
Mira's Malhar · 124
Mitra · 22
Mohini · 33
moksha · 8, 27, 61
Mother Goddess · 24
Mount Mandara · 31
Mount Meru · 8, 31, 40, 88, 94
Mughal period · 55, 97, 102-103, 114
muhurta · 110
Muslim · 47, 70-71, 97-98, 120
Mysore painting · 104, 114

N

Nabhija · 8
Nacciyar Tirumoli · **106-107**
Nagara · 88
Narada · 64, **83-86**
Narayana · 8, 44, 83, 128
Narayaneeyam · **126-128**
nata-mandir · 89
Nataraja · 74, 96

navarasa · 114
Nayanar · **69-70**
Neelakanta · 33
Noah · 19
North Star · 65

O

Odyssey · 53
Om · 2, 64

P

Padmanabhaswamy Temple · 78
Pahari painting · 103-104, 114
Pala school (Bengal) · 102-103
Pali · 69
Pandava · 59
Paramahamsa · 10, 27, 71, 96
Paramahamsa, Ramakrishna · 10
Paramavishnuloka · 93
Parijata · 32
Parvati · 33, 40, 75, 78
Pashupati · 56
Pattachitra · 104
Paurava · 49
Periyalvar · **105-107**
Pew Research Center · 51
Pitamaha · 8
Pitambara · 61
Plato · 113
Polaris · 63, 65

polestar · 65-66
Poonthanam · 68, 81, **125-128**
Porus · **48-49**
Prahlada · 65, 83
Prajapati · 5, 8, 26
pralaya · 3, **11**, 13, 19
Prambanan Temple · 8
puja · 75, 110
Purana · 10, 23, 52-54, 78
   Bhagavata · 29, 40, 54, 70, 79, 126-128
   Padma · 60
   Skanda · 60
   Vishnu · 29, 45, 54, 79, 86
   Vishnudharmottara · 98
Purushottama · 79
Pushkalavati · 48
Pushkar · 8

Q

Queen Cleophis · 48-49

R

raga
   Bhairava · 117
   Deepak · 117
   Hindola · 117
   Megha · 117
   Shri · 117
   Todi · 117

ragamala · 102, **113-118**
ragaputra · 117
   Vinoda · 117
ragini · 117
   Madhumadhavi · 117
Rahu · 33
Rahuketu · 33
Raina Beeti Jaaye (song) · 117-118
Raj, Bhoj · 121-122
Rajasthani painting · 103, 114
Rajneesh · 119
Rajput painting · 103
Rama · 8, 26, 43, 53, 70, 75, 77, 79, 132-133
Ramanathaswamy Temple · 77, 132-133
Ramanuja · 61
Ramayana · 53, 70, 95, 103, 107, 132
Rambha · 32
Rameswaram · 77, 131-133
Ranganatha · 106-107
Ranganathaswamy Temple · 87, 89, 91, 96, 106
rasa · **114**
Rasa lila · 122
rasika · 114
Ratha Yatra · 76
Ravana · 43, 77, 132
Rigveda · 22
rishi · 11, 13
Rudra · 53, 56, 62
Rukmini · 43
Russian sunflower · 2

S

Sagan, Carl · 15
Sahasranama · 59-62
Sambandar · 69
samsara · 21, 27
samudra manthan (See churning of the milky ocean) · **29**
Santhana Gopala · 126-127
Saptarishis · 19
Sarah · 5
Saraswati · 5, 7-8, 10
sati · 122
Saura (sect) · 23
Semitic religion · 25
Seven Rishis · 18
Shah Jahan · 98
Shaivism · 55
Shaivite · 23, 41, 62, 69, 70, 80, 128
Shakta · 69
Shakti · 4, 9, 24
Shaktism · 53, 55
Shamas, Victor · 62
Shankara · 61, 132
Shankaranarayana · 62
Shastra · 52
Shatapatha Brahmana · 20
Shatarupa · 7, 19
shikhara · **88-89**
Shilanidhi · 84, 86
Shirdi Sai Baba Temple · 77
Shishupala · 41, 42, 43, 68

Shiva · 1, 3, 5-9, 11, 15, 21-24, 26, 30-31, 33, 35-37, 39-40, 42-43, 53, 56, 62, 69, 70, 74-78, 83-86, 88-89, 92, 96, 98, 104, 117, 132-133
Siddhivinayak Temple · 77
Sikandar · 49
Sir John Marshall · 100
Sittanavasal · 99
Sivananda, Swami · 37, 131
Smarta · 24, 69
soma · 43, 67
Somnath Temple · 77
Sri · 56, 80
Srimati · 84-86
Srivatsa · 44
stotra · 60, 126
stupa · 74
Sudarshana Chakra · 33, 44
Sufi · 71
Sun Temple of Konark · 87, 89-90
Sundarar · 69
Surdas · 117
Surya · 17, 22-24, 44
Suryavarman II · 93-94
Sutra · 52
Swami Prabhupada · 80-81
Swami Tapasyananda · 61
Swaminarayan Akshardham Temple · 87, 90-91, 93, 96
swan · 7, 9-10, 36
Swayambhuva Manu · 19
swayamvara · 84-86

T

Taj Mahal · 98
Taliban · 47
tandava · 1
Tanjore · 102, 104
Tendulkar, Sachin · 39
Thommanon · 93-94
Thoreau, Henry David · 66
tilak · 80
tirthankara · 74
Tirumala Venkateswara Temple · 76
Tiruppavai · 106-107
Trikuta Mountains · 77
Trimurti · 5, 8, **21-24**, 35, 37, 41, 43, 83
Trinity · 21, 24, 74
Tripundra · 80
Tukaram · 70, 81
Tulsi · 70, 81, 105
Twain, Mark · 17
Tyagaraja · 1

U

Uchchaihsravas · 32
Udayagiri · 55
UNESCO World Heritage · 23, 87, 99
Upanishad · 26-27, 69
    Shvetashvatara · 53, 68, 71
Uttanapada · 63
Uttarakhand · 132-133

V

Vac · 7
Vaikuntha · 40, 42, 75
Vaishnava · 23, 29, 35, 37, 40, 43, 55, 61, 62, 69, 79, 80-81, 94, 103, 105, 107, 120, 125, 128, 133
Vaishnavism · 55, **79-81**
Vaishnavite · 79-80
Vaishno Devi Temple · 77
Vaitheeswaran Koil · 96
Vaivasvata Manu · 19
Vallabha · 70
Vamana · 43
Varaha · 55
varna · 7, 52
Varuna · 22, 32
Varuni · 32
Vasu · 65-66
Vasudeva · 44
Vasuki · 31, 34
Vayu · 22
Veda · 1, 7-8, 18, 26, 47, 51-52, 54
Vedic period · 5, 8, 20, 22, 26, 29, 43, 47, 52-54, 67, 71, 74, 79
veena · 83-85
Venkateswara · 76, 107
Vesara · 88
vibhakti · 125, 127
vimana · 88
Vishnu · 1-6, 8-10, 15, 19, 21-24, 26, 30-33, 35-37, **39-45**, 53-56, 59-62, 64-65, 68-70, 74-80, 83-86, 92-96, 105-107, 117, 120, 122, 127, 132-133
Vishnu Sahasranama · 44, **59-62**
Voltaire · 5
Vrindavan · 122-123
Vritra · 43

W

wall painting · 99
Wat Athvea · 93-94
Watts, Alan · 4

Y

Yamunotri · 133
Yogananda, Paramahamsa · 10, 71
Yudhishthira · 59, 60
yuga · 7, **11-13**
　Dvapara · 12
　Kali · 12-13
　Satya · 12
　Treta · 12

What's Next?

That's me, Sach, performing an Ananda Sayana outdoors. Having completed more than a quarter of our journey, I believe we are due for a well-deserved break. While Vishnu's cosmic sleep goes on for *yugas*, ours will be a short *sayana*.

But Vishnu is not known to be a sleeping beauty, either. When he's awake, he occasionally turns into an cosmic undercover law enforcement agent—or avatar, as we call it—and strives to restore world order and peace. Some readers may be familiar with Dashavataras, or the ten avatars of Vishnu. They are in fact the top ten avatars of Vishnu. According to the Bhagavata Purana, Vishnu had twenty-two avatars. Other texts mention twenty-four or thirty-nine. Like everything in Hinduism, this number keeps changing. Even the Dashavataras are not consistent and have variations, but fortunately they are small.

By the way, have you already forgotten some of the characters we have met so far? If so, don't worry because we will meet them again. In the next two books of this series, we enter the most exciting part of our journey—The Dashavataras—where we focus on not only the many forms of Vishnu but the epics Ramayana and Mahabharata. And guess what? When you read these tales, our lives in the planet may seem so boring. Stay tuned.

If you enjoyed reading this book,
please take a moment to leave a review.

Much appreciated and thank you.

www.ingramcontent.com/pod-product-compliance
Lightning Source LLC
Chambersburg PA
CBHW020653300426
44112CB00007B/363